The unauthorized reproduction or distribution of a copyrighted work is illegal. Criminal copyright infringement, including infringement without monetary gain, is investigated by the FBI and is punishable by fines and federal imprisonment.

Please purchase only authorized editions and do not participate in or encourage, the piracy of copyrighted material. Your support of author's rights is appreciated.

This book is a work of fiction. Names, characters, places and incidents are the products of the author's imagination or used fictitiously. Any resemblance to actual events, locales or persons, living or dead is entirely coincidental.

Release: Masters of the Savoy copyrighted 2022 by Delta James

---

Want FREE books from Delta James?

Go to https://www.subscribepage.com/VIPlist22019 to sign up for Delta James' newsletter and receive a copy of *Harvest* along with several other free stories. In addition to the free stories you will also get access to bonus stories, sales, giveaways and news of new releases.

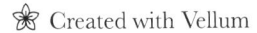

✾ Created with Vellum

RELEASE: MASTERS OF THE SAVOY
A SUPERNATURAL MYSTERY AND ROMANCE

DELTA JAMES

ACKNOWLEDGEMENTS: *These things are so hard to write. It can't be as long as the book, but you fear leaving people out. So instead, I'll just go with the basics:*

- *To my father who gave me the gift of storytelling*
- *To Renee and Chris, without whom none of what I do would be possible*
- *To the Girls: Goody, Katy, Emma, Roz, Ava and Skylar*
- *To Kathy, Autumn and Melinda Kaye—thanks for having my back*
- *To my Critical Reader and Focus Groups, JT Farrell and all of my readers – thank you from the bottom of my heart*
- *To Andrea Neil of Three Point Author Services, for all her hard work*
- *To Dar Albert of Wicked Smart Designs, the genius behind my covers who works with nothing from me and produces the most amazing artwork, which then become my covers*

CHAPTER 1

Year of Our Lord 1539
Castle Tremayne
Cornish Coast, England

The night was upon him. Tremayne could feel the shackles of the curse releasing their stony hold on him. For more than two centuries, Holden Tremayne had been confined to his own personal hell. There were times Tremayne could see a kind of poetic justice in damning him to a half-life where he only *lived* during the darkest hours of the night while most others slept. It was then and only then that the granite cracked, crumbled, and fell away, releasing him once more into the world.

But it was a world that had changed vastly from the time before. Before he had been cursed and damned to hold an eternal vigil through unseeing eyes, he had been one of the privileged. He'd lived as he pleased. The son of the Duke of Cornwall, his days had been filled with fighting, drinking and wenching, activities in which he had excelled. It was the last of those behaviors that had damned him to the existence he now endured.

The girl had been a tavern wench, nothing more than a casual dalliance—a one-time thing to ease the lust that was riding him hard after a day of hunting and drinking with his friends. He hadn't forced her to his bed, nor had he known she was a virgin until he shattered the shield of her maidenhood as he thrust up into her.

Six months later she'd appeared outside the castle walls, pregnant, standing on the cliff as the wind off the ocean roared its fury at what he'd done. When Holden had refused to marry her—after all, he might have been the first, but he hadn't been the last—the girl had backed to the edge of the precipice, extended her arms out to her sides and simply tumbled backward to her death.

That night, just before sunset, her elder sister had appeared, lighting a great bonfire in the same spot. As the flames had spit and crackled, dancing with the stars and the storm that swirled all around her, she pointed to Holden who stood on the battlements of the castle and called:

> You who dimmed the light that shone
> Shall be forever cast in stone
> To watch by day and live by night
> Your cursed life can only be undone
> When your devotion to the Light has begun

Then the tower of fire seemed to explode, and when it settled again to nothing more than a beacon of light, the witch had disappeared.

Holden had laughed it off as nothing more than the raving of a grief-stricken sister. He went to his bed and slowly came awake before dawn to the sound of the curse being whispered in his ear. He opened his eyes with a start, grabbing the dagger he kept under his pillow. Rolling away from the sound, he got to his feet on the other side of the bed.

Seeing nothing, he said angrily, "Who are you? Show yourself!"

There was no response as Holden quieted his breathing. He shot a look at the door and saw that the bolt was still locked in place. He made a thorough search of his chambers and when he found no one there, he pulled on his shirt, breeches, and boots.

Perhaps something to eat might soothe his nerves. He unbolted the door and wandered from his suite of rooms upstairs down to the kitchens where work had started long before the darkness had begun to fade.

"You're up awfully early," said Agatha, the head cook. "The sun hasn't even begun to rise."

"Bad dreams. I need some ale and maybe a chunk of that bread you just brought out of the oven."

Agatha shook her head. "You've had a nose for fresh bread since you were a boy. Wesley, get the Marquess a tankard of ale."

The kitchen boy went to do as she asked while Agatha tore off a sizeable chunk of bread for Holden and slathered sweet-cream butter all over it. She handed the bread to him and Holden tore off a chunk with his even, white teeth, enjoying the way the melted butter dribbled down his chin only to be wiped away with the cuff of his shirt.

"I'm going back up to the battlements to clear my head."

"Then perhaps it should be something other than ale that you're breaking your fast with."

"Nay, Agatha, your good bread and this fine ale will see me put right."

Holden made his way up to the great stone pathway that topped the walls. The walls, the turrets, and the location of the castle itself gave them a strategic advantage when any tried to attack or lay siege to them. There were also hidden tunnels and escape routes leading both inland and to the sea. Castle Tremayne had never been breached.

He breathed in deeply as he put his shoulder into the heavy oak door and made his way outside. The sea was still up, and he could hear it crashing against the sea cliff and the rocks below. The wind whipped and howled through the castle. He passed the spot where the bonfire had blazed on the open field outside the castle walls. He could still remember the woman shouting her curse, backlit by the flames. It had been, if he was being honest with himself, a bit unnerving.

Holden finished the bread and ale, setting the tankard on the inner ledge of the battlement and laughed when the wailing wind swept it from its precarious perch. He proceeded to the middle of the walkway where he could stand facing the sea full on. One of his younger brothers had gone to sea, after his father had purchased him a commission in the Navy. His middle brother was studying to become a barrister.

And his sister, who often gave Holden a run for his money in being an embarrassment to their father, had refused the marriage their father had arranged and instead ran off and joined the Order of the Seven Maidens. Now there was a group of intriguing women. They weren't exactly nuns, as the Church had disavowed them, but they weren't exactly typical women, either.

They lived their lives on their own in a self-sustaining community, selling the honey, mead and wool they produced and didn't need for themselves. The women of the original Order had rebuilt a cloister that had been ravaged by Viking raiders. Over the centuries, they had expanded and updated their home. Vowing to depend on no one other than themselves, they became experts in the sword and bow and had beaten back more than one group of men intent on breaching their walls.

In a gross imitation of the pregnant girl's stance right before she'd tumbled from the ledge of the cliff to the sea and rocks below, Holden held his arms straight out, level with his shoulders, and tossed his head back, drinking in the morning sun as it rose and laughing at what the day might bring.

Suddenly his feet and then his legs began to feel heavy and stiff. He looked down and watched as stone seemed to grow up from the walkway to encase his legs and rise higher with each passing moment. In an instant of understanding, Holden realized with horror that his legs weren't being enclosed by the advancing granite but were instead becoming solid rock themselves. His cock stiffened and lifted, almost touching his navel as the stone continued to consume his body. His feet had become cloven hooves and it was growing difficult to breathe.

The witch's curse was coming true. As the sun rose, Holden was becoming cast in stone. The granite moved up his torso and he could feel something springing from his spine. He had just enough time to glance over his shoulder and see spikes erupting from his back. A painful feeling rose from his head and below his jawline. His head became misshapen, resembling that of a dragon of old, and ridges grew along the sides and back of his hairline like a bony frill. Before he could scream, his face froze in a horrified expression and blackness descended, gripping him with fear that he would be this way forever.

The first time he awakened, he was in a garden he had never seen before. Holden could feel the granite begin to crumble and fall away. A full moon shone overhead, and he was cold.

"Thank God you're awake," said his sister, Morwenna, as he opened his eyes trying to adjust to the darkness. "Imagine yourself as you have always been—my handsome, strong, and good brother."

"There are those who would doubt that last one."

"Then they would be wrong," she said, coming to stand beside him. He and Morwenna had always been close.

"Where am I?" he said, testing his limbs and taking a tentative step toward her.

His legs felt leaden, but they worked. He glanced to check the state of his spines.

"The wings…"

"I have wings?"

"Aye, they come out of your shoulder blades, and it looks as though you could fly with them. You can fold them over the spikes when you become the gargoyle. We've done some research on the curse that was laid on you." She reached out to touch his shoulder. "We believe you have the ability to shift between your two selves—man and gargoyle. Although the legends say you will always shift to a gargoyle before you turn to stone. If you can think of yourself as human, the wings, spikes, horns, and ridges will all recede into your body. It seems as though, dear brother, the thing that got you into this mess refuses to behave." She said the last with a laugh.

Holden looked down. She was right; his unruly cock still stood at attention, pressing against the front of his breeches. While somewhat embarrassing, he was grateful the damn thing was still there.

"Morwenna, where am I?" he said, looking around and not recognizing any of the landscape before him.

"You are in the Order's meditation garden. Before you fly off the handle and demand a horse to take you home, you should know father and those in the village have judged you accursed and had planned to smash you into bits and throw you into the sea."

"What?" he asked, quickly looking around.

Morwenna nodded. "Even though your head and parts of your body were misshapen, it was clear who you were and that you had been cursed. They tried to find the one who did this to you, but she had cleared out of her croft and vanished." She shook her head. "You've really done it this time."

He looked around at the garden, taking in the variety of plants and herbs that grew along its borders. "How did I get here?"

"Agatha found you and sent for me. She was

afraid of what they might do to you. By the time father discovered you and got the men and tools assembled to ensure your destruction, those in the Order had followed me to the castle through the tunnels. We persuaded those of father's men he'd left to guard you to let us take you."

"At sword point?" he asked, arching his brow. The women of the Order were notorious for being fearless.

"We find it easier to make men see reason if we give them no other choice. Then we hauled your heavy, sorry ass to our cloister." Morwenna rose from the bench she'd been seated on and extended her arm to him. "Come along, Holden. I don't know about you, but I'm cold and hungry."

His belly growled in agreement as he fell in beside her and crossed a threshold that no man had crossed in centuries. "How long have I been asleep?"

"Not long. Just the day. It would seem you turn to stone as the sun rises and when it sets, the stone crumbles to dust."

Holden would always be grateful to his sister. He had remained with the Order long after her death and the death of those who had fought to protect him as he slept. He'd watched over them from behind the sacred walls of the cloister or from overhead as he soared through the sky during the darkest part of the night in his altered form. He had lived long past what anyone would consider normal and had watched the world change—some of it good; some of it not so good.

He'd long ago recognized that what he experienced during the day wasn't really sleep, but rather a kind of suspended animation. Holden woke refreshed and healed from any wound or injury, but he missed the comfort of a bed. The kind of life he had so often eschewed had become his most fervent desire. As time passed, he sought the company of humans less and less. The pain of losing those he came to care about began to wear on his soul and it was easier to avoid any kind of true attachment.

The years had also brought regret. He had long ago forgiven the witch who had cursed him. In fact, he wasn't sure he didn't agree with what she had done. Was the babe her sister took with her over the cliff his? Doubtful, but turning his back on her had been cold and cavalier. The girl had thrown herself from the cliff because she felt she had no options and he had certainly not given her any.

He often thought if he could have changed one thing in his past, it wouldn't be that he'd been cursed to live as something far from human. No, the thing he would have changed would have been how he'd treated the girl. Regardless of what she had done or what she had accused him of, she deserved better. Holden often thought that becoming a gargoyle had made him a better man.

Over the centuries, Holden had learned how to

shift between man and beast and sometimes into something in between. He could control what manifested and what didn't as he came awake, but each morning as the stone began its crawl up his body, the gargoyle came to the fore, and he would remain a stone grotesque for as long as the sun made its way across the sky. If, as some of the prophets and astrologists predicted, the sun should set, never to rise again, he might be free of part of his curse, but he wondered how long he could maintain his human form without rest.

As the Age of Man progressed and industrialization began to erode the ancient way of life in Cornwall, Holden had realized he was a threat to the Order that had protected him for centuries. Deciding that London and other large cities with Gothic architecture would allow him to hide in plain sight, he had made a home for himself amongst the other gargoyles, grotesques, and saints in Cardiff, Paris, London and the like, where no one noticed an additional stone statue.

There had been a clan of gargoyles that ruled London during the reign of Queen Victoria. They had all but beaten him to death one night when he'd crossed their path. They had deemed him unfit, as he was not a pureblood, but rather some misbegotten bastardization of their kind called cursedborn. After that he had kept to himself, living a life mostly of solitude… until he met her.

CHAPTER 2

Present Day
London, England

Mazie Bridges paced back and forth in front of the rather nondescript door at 221A Baker Street. The only signage was immediately under the address, and it read *Cerberus Group*. She'd done her research and knew that the famed 'lifestyle club' only took up two of the floors of the building. The third was occupied by the headquarters of one of the best K&R firms in the world. The head of Cerberus, Robert Fitzwallace, was married to JJ Fitzwallace, who was both an international activist and the proprietor of the club.

Baker Street was the club at which Anne and Gabe Watson played. Gabriel Watson had been her boss at the Savoy. He'd hired her when Scotland Yard hadn't. Gabe was one of the nicest, hunkiest guys she'd ever known. He and Anne had emigrated to America. Mazie had become fascinated with both the lifestyle and the club. The women she most admired, mostly from afar, were all involved with both. She'd begun doing research and in the past few weeks she had talked about it to both Anne and her friend Corinne, who was the part-time night concierge of the hotel.

For her birthday, Anne and Gabe had gifted her with a guest pass and sponsorship to the club if she chose to pursue a D/s lifestyle. Anne had gone so far as to drag her off to a custom corsetier and help her purchase her first corset and matching boy shorts. So, now, she was here on the street outside the club, pacing back and forth. Part of her wanted to pick up and run back to her *pied-á-terre* at the top of the row house in Notting Hill. The other part wanted to open that door and take a chance that maybe this was the thing she'd always been missing. The fact was that her family would have been aghast at her even considering such an option.

"Hello," said a gorgeous woman with dark hair. She was dressed in a killer outfit—a black leather pencil skirt, black silk tank and an *avant-garde* jacket. Mazie was convinced if she'd tried to walk in the stiletto heels the woman was wearing, she'd break an ankle. "Can I help you?"

"I'm not sure. My friends gave me a guest pass, but I just don't think I'd fit in," replied Mazie.

"Whyever not? I like to think Baker Street is the most accepting, nonjudgmental place in the world."

"Are you a member?" Mazie asked.

"Member? I suppose. I'm JJ Fitzwallace; I own the joint. A guest pass and a little unsure of yourself—you must be Anne and Gabe's friend, Mazie."

Mazie nodded, stunned the woman knew her name as she wondered what Gabe and Anne must have said that had made a woman like JJ Fitzwallace remember her.

Linking her arm through Mazie's, JJ led her toward the door. "Come on. The club is just getting ready to open for the night. How about I buy you a drink and give you a private tour?"

"I wouldn't want you to waste your time," said Mazie. She was still unsure of what to do, but her feet kept moving her toward the door.

"It's my time to do what I like with and introducing someone to the lifestyle is never a waste, especially if it's a gorgeous sub like you. The unattached Doms are going to eat you up, but not to worry, the others will keep them at bay. And in D/s, the sub is the one with the power. I'm sorry, that was rude," she said, dragging Mazie inside the club with her. "Do you know enough to know if you identify as a Dom or a sub?"

Mazie laughed and began to relax. She felt with JJ as she most often did with Anne—that she was in the presence of a woman of great life experience and kindness.

"I think I'd be a sub, don't you?" asked Mazie.

"I think this is Baker Street, and you can be anything you want to be."

"Are you a Domme?"

From behind them came a rumbling laugh and the sound of a hand smacking leather as a deep Scottish brogue said, "She likes to think so every now and again."

"Shit, Fitz."

The towering hunk of a man hauled JJ into his arms, kissed her soundly and said, "That's five you owe me, lassie."

"Behave yourself or poor Mazie will go running out of here cursing the day she ever met Anne and Gabe," said JJ, wrapping her arm around his waist. "Mazie… Bridges, wasn't it?" Mazie nodded, fascinated by the body language between the two. "I'd like you to meet my husband, Robert Fitzwallace."

"Oh yes, you work, or rather worked, for Gabe over at the Savoy. He says you're one of the best hackers—computer security people—he's ever known. Cerberus is always looking for good people. If the Savoy doesn't treat you right, you come talk to me before you take a job anywhere else. Deal?"

Mazie found herself nodding. "Sure."

Maybe this night won't be a total bust!

"Fitz, I promised to buy Mazie a drink and show

her around. I'm sure Anne explained to you that you can't play unless you take the classes, which are included in your membership, or you're a member of a club with whom we have reciprocity."

"Yes, she did."

"Good. First rule—you're not allowed anywhere beyond those French doors if you aren't in fet wear. The staircase leads up to the private play areas and the elevator will take you to the top floor where Fitz keeps his group. We keep all kinds of things for guests in all kinds of sizes, so we'll get you fixed up."

"Even for someone like me?" Mazie asked.

Mazie wasn't fat, not even chubby, really, but she carried a few extra pounds, and was short. She wore her dark hair in a pixie cut and tended to dress in comfortable clothes—which Anne had called baggy and dreadful—and sensible shoes.

"And what would you mean by someone like you?" asked Fitzwallace in the same deep, dark tone she'd heard Anne refer to as his 'Dom voice.'

"Fitz, she's new to the lifestyle, cut her a little slack. Second rule, subs don't talk down about their appearance, or their Dom or one of the resident Doms will administer some kind of discipline." JJ reached up and pressed her lips against Fitz's. "Please?"

The Scotsman said nothing but nodded before he hauled his wife's body up against his. "You'd best get changed as well, Mrs. Fitzwallace. I have a bit of paperwork to do, but I should be down in an hour." He turned to Mazie. "Don't let my beautiful brat lead you astray. If you have questions, best to ask one of the Doms."

Fitzwallace kissed his wife again, patting her backside. Just like with Gabe and Anne, you could practically feel the connection between the two. Mazie couldn't imagine ever having that with anyone. Regardless of what Fitzwallace or any of the rest said, Mazie knew that her looks didn't stack up against someone like Anne or JJ, or any of the other women that passed them to go through the French doors. Although as they entered the actual club, Mazie could see there were women of all shapes and sizes.

"Come on Mazie, let's go see what we can find for you to wear. If you're interested, I can give you the name of a couple of really good corsetiers."

"Actually, as part of my birthday present, Anne took me to this amazing place called the Dark Garden."

"You mean she and Gabe took you," said JJ, leading Mazie through the doors and turning down a hallway.

"No, just me and Anne. Why would Gabe come to a corset shop?"

JJ Fitzwallace looked gobsmacked. "You mean to tell me that you bought something at Dark Garden without a Dom in attendance?" Mazie nodded. "That little prick. I swear I'm going to murder him."

"Please don't. I wasn't supposed to tell," explained Mazie, hoping she hadn't committed a *faux pas* so great that she would be barred from a lifestyle that was starting to become more attractive. "I'm sorry."

"You have nothing to apologize for. I swear Anne can get people to do just about anything for her. I'm not angry, I just want to know her secret. Come on."

The façade of Baker Street betrayed nothing of what lay beyond its outer door—the only signs on the brick exterior were the address, 221A, and a small sign that indicated it was the headquarters of Cerberus, an elite security firm.

Inside and to the left of the reception desk, an elaborate set of French doors barred the way from non-members even being given a glimpse into the inner sanctum—warm wood paneling of the Victorian era graced the walls in the halls and lounge. The dungeon floor had the same kind of ornate paneling as wainscotting with beautifully plastered walls.

On the other side of the French doors was another reception area, featuring an ornate set of stairs that led to the second, third and top floors, as well as a small hall that held two elevators and served as a pass-through to the club's lounge. The reception desk inside the club proper was manned by a beautiful woman dressed in an elegant steampunk outfit.

To the right lay the main dungeon, with three smaller, more intimate scening areas on that same floor as well as changing rooms for men and women.

The Submissives' Salon was luxe—with comfortable chairs and chaises, armoires instead of lockers and elaborate showers and two clawfoot tubs.

They stepped into the decadent submissives' salon. Mazie felt like she'd fallen down the rabbit hole into a steampunk wonderland. The lockers were actually small armoires made of beautifully polished wood. The actual dressing room was paneled in Victorian paneling, and she could see the shower area that lay beyond was floor-to-ceiling white subway tile.

"This is gorgeous," whispered Mazie.

"Thank you. I am rather proud of it. The showers are back there and over to the left is a place to do your makeup and hair. I had special lighting installed. So, let's see what Louis made for you. Do you need a hand getting into your corset?"

"Yes, please. You know, Anne said everyone here was so nice and I'm beginning to think she was right."

JJ smiled warmly and showed her to an armoire where Mazie could stow her gear. All the feelings she would get in gym class came up. Stripping down to nothing created a level of fear which she was all too familiar with. But she knew that here at Baker Street, that kind of thinking could get a girl disciplined. The Doms were not inclined to let submissives speak ill of themselves.

"Nobody will judge you. Ask someone for an opinion about how a corset looks, and they'll tell you. Otherwise, they won't care. I know for some of us, getting naked or almost naked can be a bit awkward. I need to attend to something out front, so I'll leave you alone for a bit."

Mazie looked around and all the women in the salon were in various stages of undress. She stripped out of her clothes, keeping her bra on while she pulled on her black leather boy shorts. She pulled at the back of them—the damn things didn't cover her ass adequately.

When JJ returned, Mazie said "Maybe I should borrow something for the bottom. I don't think these fit."

JJ spun her around. "Oh, they fit just fine. You have a great ass. It's going to drive a lot of the Doms nuts. Come on, get out of that bra and we'll get you laced up." JJ picked up the ruby-red corset with a black lace overlay. "The man may be a jerk, but he does beautiful work. Subs can wear heels or bare feet. Dommes wear boots."

"If I tried to walk in heels like you have on, I'd break something."

JJ laughed. "They take some practice, but honestly most of us go barefoot. It's just easier. Raise your arms over your head and I'll pull the corset on and help you get it adjusted. Once we've got everything situated where you want it, I'll lace you up."

Mazie unhooked her bra, slipped out of it, and hung it in the armoire. She turned to face JJ, who helped her shimmy into the corset. Once Mazie had her boobs where they belonged, JJ spun her around and started lacing her up.

"Breathe out, I won't lace you up too tight. You might want to stay in it just for a couple of hours. If you start to feel lightheaded or nauseous, let someone know and they can loosen the laces for you. There's a reason women who wore these things used to have the vapors."

Mazie laughed and then groaned as JJ tightened the corset. JJ took her into the hair and makeup area and helped polish off the look. When she turned Mazie around, Mazie found it hard to believe the curvy, attractive woman staring back from the mirror was her.

"Don't you ever tell Fitz I said this, but mostly the Doms are right. We women are champions at tearing ourselves down. Now let's go get that drink."

JJ led her out of the salon and to the club's bar, which resembled a Victorian gentleman's smoking lounge, even though there was no smoke. The whole place was a feast for the eyes. The lounge overlooked the dungeon floor and main scening area.

Mazie's eyes went wide as she watched a tall, muscular man bind a gorgeous, naked blonde with long curly hair to a large contraption that resembled a large letter *X*.

"That's a St. Andrew's Cross, right?" she asked JJ.

"Very good. You've been doing your research. Is this your first time in a dungeon?" Mazie nodded.

"That's Sawyer," JJ said, pointing to the mass of muscles. "He is a whip master. The woman with him is his wife and sub, Rhiannon. I'm so glad you're getting to see them for your first time."

The man removed his leather vest, revealing a cut chest and six-pack abs. He fisted the woman's hair, tilting her head back and kissing her before drawing her golden tresses up onto the top of her head to ensure they would be out of the way. He stepped back, unfurling a flogger with a number of falls ending in small, braided knots, and swung it gently back and forth. There was a predatory grace in the way he moved; he was obviously comfortable with both the flogger and the woman tied to the cross. There was no sound as the man brought the flogger down across the woman's ivory skin. Her entire body seemed to tremble as subtle pink lines marred her pale flesh.

"Sawyer knows what he's doing. With a master like him, all Rhiannon feels is a lovely thud followed by the most delicious warmth," explained JJ. "That is, when he's not disciplining her."

Mazie continued to watch, fascinated by what she was seeing.

"Rhiannon loves the whip, whether it's the flogger or the single tail. Watch her body language. See how she's a bit tense? She and Sawyer just returned from an intense work assignment. Sawyer will use the flogger until her whole body is relaxed and she sags against the cross."

"You sound like you speak from experience," said Mazie.

"Fitz is a whip master as well. He once told me that making me sub out and then caring for me makes him feel necessary, like there's more to his life than just violence. Even if that violence is in the name of protecting the innocent."

Mazie was mesmerized by the rhythmic rise and fall of the flogger. Each time the falls landed, several more marks rose on Rhiannon's flesh, but never broke it. At first, Rhiannon had appeared stiff, but ultimately her body began to relax until she was leaning, or as JJ had said, sagging against the piece of equipment. Mazie watched as Sawyer stepped closer to her, murmuring something in her ear as he nuzzled her neck. He released the bindings and helped her off the cross. Sawyer was handed a blanket and wrapped it lovingly around his wife before scooping her up and cradling her in his arms. He spoke to the person who'd handed him the blanket and then left the area headed for the lounge.

"Harry will clean up for him so Sawyer can look after Rhiannon. Even though they're members and both work for Fitz, the rules say she needs to come out of subspace before they can leave to go home," said JJ.

Sawyer entered the bar with Rhiannon snuggled

in his arms. He picked one of the large wingback chairs in the back of the lounge where the light was much dimmer. He continued to speak quietly and soothingly to Rhiannon until her body was completely relaxed and her breathing deepened and evened out as she fell asleep.

Mazie leaned over to JJ. "Sign me up."

CHAPTER 3

The following week, Mazie sat in what was affectionately referred to by staff as the 'command center.' It was a small room filled mostly with computers, monitors, and a bank of desks that formed a semi-circle. The interior of the circle held three chairs in a pinch, but rarely no more than two were ever used. The person monitoring the two screens could switch from one to another with the flip of a switch or movement of a mouse. The computers were an integral part of the Savoy's security system and recorded data and images gleaned from the cameras strategically placed within the hotel. The room had no windows and only one exit door, which was kept locked and required a key card with the proper security level encoded.

Right now, Mazie was the only one on duty monitoring the systems. There were other security personnel on staff who roamed the hotel and were available for dispatch, but at the moment she was the only one on the day shift. Gabriel Watson's *bon voyage* and *bon chance* party had been almost a week ago. Mazie had been surprised when Felix Spenser, the head concierge, had arranged it. She had thought management would be upset that Gabe was leaving, but Spense had said while they didn't like losing him, they'd wanted him to know he was appreciated.

No one was sorrier to see Gabe go than Mazie. Rumor had been rife that the Biltmore Hotel had lured him away. Mazie knew it wasn't true. He'd confided to her that he and Anne had purchased Sage Matthews' home on the Outer Banks of North Carolina, and that he and the members of his old unit were starting up an investigative and protection service they'd named Steel Knights Investigations. She wished them both well, but she would miss them dearly.

Scanning the monitors, she noticed a man coming out of a stairwell. He was dressed in a very nondescript way in a pair of dark trousers and T-shirt, which revealed well-defined, muscular arms. A cap with a visor was pulled down low over his eyes. The real kicker, though, was the dark gloves.

Opening a communication channel, she spoke. "Donny, head to the sixth floor. I've got my eye on a guy who just came out of the stairwell. He looks like he's trying to avoid the cameras."

"On my way," came the response.

Within moments, Donny had exited the lift on the sixth floor and spotted the man at the end of the hall, standing in front of the door to an exclusive suite. Mazie watched Donny hail the man. Instead of running, he turned to confront Donny. Mazie was poised with her hand over the panic button, which would send the others in the security detail to Donny's location, seal the elevator doors, and lock the stairwell door to everyone without security authorization.

The man removed his hat, holding it in front of his lower body, and explained something to Donny. Mazie zoomed the security camera in on the man's hands. He was clutching his cap but kept his hands moving around the brim. The guy was nervous. He handed Donny his identification and showed him the key card for the room. Donny seemed satisfied, gave the all clear signal and headed for the elevator.

Mazie waited until Donny was in the lift. "Well?"

"It seems Mr. Fremont and his wife are guests here and were playing naughty games. He was supposed to break in, tie her to the bed, and have his way with her," Donny replied, laughing.

She ran the name through the electronic guest register and confirmed that Mr. and Mrs. Fremont were the guests assigned to that room.

"I told him that he might not want to be skulking

around the hotel looking suspicious," continued Donny.

"He looked a bit sheepish, but not upset."

"He wasn't the least bit annoyed. In fact, he was pretty impressed that we caught him and responded so quickly. So good on you."

"That's what we're here for. Thanks for checking it out."

"Just doing my job, Mazie, just doing my job. I get off at six tonight. Any chance you'd let me buy you a drink?"

"Thanks, Donny, but I have plans. I'm sorry."

"Okay, sure. I understand," he said, but his voice said he didn't.

For the most part, Mazie didn't date and she sure as hell didn't date coworkers. She was happy to go out with a group, but she preferred to keep her work separate from her personal life. Mostly she spent her off time preparing for a real-life version of her favorite video game, Castle Reign, and most recently exploring the lifestyle and pleasures of Baker Street.

Mazie had come to the Savoy via a failed attempt to join Scotland Yard's Cybercrime Unit. She was smart, could crack just about any code, was more comfortable with computers than most people, and had been top of her class in marksmanship. When DSI Holmes had learned that the Yard hadn't hired her, he recommended her to Gabriel Watson, the Chief of Security for the Savoy Hotel, who'd offered her a position heading up their cyber security group. She'd seen the job at the prestigious hotel as something to pay the bills until she could reapply to the Yard, but that had been more than three years ago.

Mazie had found a home here. She was comfortable and enjoyed being able to come to work, do her job well, and go home. She was a bit of a stay at home and had never equated loneliness with being alone. That wasn't to say she didn't enjoy going out with friends for a movie or a meal or just a bit of fun, but mostly she traveled between her *pied-à-terre* in Notting Hill to her job at the Savoy and back again.

It was in her small, cozy home at the top of one of the rowhouses where she'd found her true calling—not as a member of Scotland Yard, and not as a member of the Savoy's security team, but as Knight Fury, her avatar in Castle Reign. Castle Reign was an RPG/ARG/MMORPG—a computer game played both online and in real life. Mazie would shake her head at that long description; there were so many acronyms in the online world. Role Playing Game, Alternate Reality Game, Massively Multiplayer Online Role-Playing Game—basically they were all just related to online and real-life gaming.

She'd chosen the name of her avatar as a kind of homage to her favorite character in a popular animated film. The game had announced a real-life quest with a cash prize. Mazie had been approached by one of the guys she knew within the online game to join the Phantom Guild—a four-player group who would band together to play and split the prize. Their Guild consisted of Silent Knight, Rook, Bishop, and herself as Knight Fury. They had yet to meet in person, but that was about to change.

Until she'd gone to Baker Street, Castle Reign had represented the most exciting part of her life. Her classes at Baker Street had shown her three things: she was most definitely a submissive; Castle Reign was not the most interesting way to spend her time; and there were men—a lot of them—who liked short, curvy women. She had opted for the immersion training, which was a more condensed, intense version of their normal three-week long, twice-per-week training course so that her training wouldn't interfere with the Guild's quest.

She wondered if the other members of her guild had to resist the temptation to use what computer skills they might have to check out the others. When Castle Reign had posted the start of a real-life quest with its prize of a half-million US dollars, Rook and Bishop, who often played the online game together, contacted her and Silent Knight to form a guild, play the quest, and win the prize.

Mazie knew all three players, or at least their avatars. She and Silent Knight often played together and worked cooperatively within the game. He—at least she thought Silent Knight was a he—was an enigmatic player whose skill and cunning were second to none. Mazie, Rook, and Bishop were all top-ranked players, but it was Silent Knight who always led the rankings. Players often conversed in game chat, but no one knew who anyone really was. For all she knew, Rook might be an eighty-year-old spinster from Norfolk. And as far as they were concerned, she might be the same. Online, it didn't matter, but playing in the real world, physical abilities would come into play.

∽

The sun had begun its descent, sinking down beyond the western horizon. Sentience returned only moments before the granite began to crack. Tremayne had picked a secluded spot atop Westminster Abbey that was in one of the few blind spots of the city and the abbey's security cameras. As the last bit of light faded into night, the stone that trapped him during the light of day began to snap and fracture, falling away as it always did. He stood, stretching and shrugging his shoulders, brushing the last of the rock off his arms and watching as it disappeared into nothing. Flexing his wings, he extended and held them out to dry. In his grotesque form his wings were either down at his sides, folded over the spikes that ran all along his spine, or extended as if he were getting ready to take flight.

Tremayne stilled his mind, sensing and feeling the currents of wind as they whipped around him. He moved the small slab of stone that covered the hole he had dug over the years to hide his few belongings. He pulled out his duffel and opened it to remove his leathers—the clothing he wore at his current club, Baker Street. Every ten years or so, he had to change his identity and find a new lifestyle club to play at. He loved the term lifestyle club. He'd heard of such clubs during his time in Cornwall, but he had never believed they existed. Maybe if he'd known about them, he could have avoided the whole curse thing and died a fat old man with a dozen children and grandchildren at his side instead of roaming the earth in his current state.

In the beginning of his lonely existence as neither man nor beast, he had hired prostitutes, but he'd eventually grown tired of their professional personae—they were paid to enjoy whatever he wanted to do to them. There was no real spark… no true feeling. He found he needed a connection, even if it was contracted for a specific period of time. That was when he'd discovered kink clubs and he had begun to learn. A century later, he held Master's rights in some of the most prestigious clubs in the world—Torch Light, Dante's, and now Baker Street.

He put the stone covering back in place and moved to a darkened enclave on the tower. He climbed up on the ledge, checked for anyone who might be able to bear witness, then fell forward, stretching his wings out to catch the wind and glide down to the street. There he folded his wings, allowing them to recede into his body, removed a sweater from his duffel, and pulled it over his head so that he once again looked fully human. Hailing a cab, he made his way to Baker Street.

His cock throbbed against his breeches. That had to be the witch's last laugh. Each night he awoke with an engorged and needy cock. A true relationship was out of the question. How could he explain to a woman, any woman, that he could only be reached after sunset and before sunrise? Most nights he either roamed the city or holed up in one of the all-night coffeehouses playing the online game Castle Reign.

He tried to refrain from sex. After all, his loose ways and disrespectful treatment of women was what had gotten him cursed. He hadn't raped the girl and there had been no evidence that he was the father of her unborn child, but as the duke's son, he was certainly the best prospect of the lot. However, he didn't blame her for what had happened to him. Hell, he didn't even blame her sister.

Most nights he worked off his primitive cravings by either immersing himself in Castle Reign or by flying over the city, searching for those he could help. He didn't hold himself up to be a hero who was doing the right thing, he was simply a monster, still trying to do penance. But there were some nights he needed. And what he needed was a woman—one who would willingly consent to allow him to control their encounter so that he could satisfy them both and serve his appetite.

Tonight, the beast within that was barely beneath the surface was hungry… and Tremayne meant to feed.

CHAPTER 4

*H*ailing a cab, he waited until it stopped, got in, and pulled out his mobile.

"Where to?" said the cabby.

"221A Baker Street."

"I'm pretty sure the Sherlock Holmes Museum is closed for the day."

Holden chuckled. "That's 221B, I'm going to the club next door."

The cabby caught Holden's eyes in his rearview mirror, raising his eyebrows in question and either disdain or rampant curiosity. Holden couldn't tell which and it really didn't matter. He ached. En route to the club, he checked his chat mail:

Rook: So, we're set to meet at the Coal Hole on the Strand tomorrow at 8?

Bishop: I've got it on my calendar.

KnightFury: I'll be there too.

SilentKnight: As will I.

Rook: I have a friend who works there. He said he'd save us a table at the back by the window. Just ask for the Phantom Guild. See you then. We're going to rock this thing.

End of Chat

He flipped off his phone and tossed it into his duffel. Within minutes, the cabby delivered him to the door of Baker Street. Holden paid the man, and then entered the building, breathing a sigh of relief as he knew he would soon get what he needed. He headed into the men's locker room. He'd been in the women's salon once and it was a lovely, feminine space that spoke of luxury and comfort. The men's locker room, on the other hand, was industrial and practical—showers, lockers, and a fridge for refreshments.

"Holden, good to see you," said Adam Wheldon, Baker Street's head of security. "It's been a while."

"Need hasn't been riding me as hard of late. Anything new I should know about?" he asked, signing in.

"Not a *thing*, exactly, but a *who* you might like very well."

Holden smiled a predatory smile. "Who might that be?"

"Mazie Bridges. I'm not sure she's ready yet for primal play, but she's new, funny, and intelligent. I'm told she's responsive as all get out. Her likes are right up your alley and she's relatively new to the lifestyle. She's up in the lounge, surrounded by a throng of admirers so she might be hard to get to."

"That won't be a problem," said Holden.

Did he say Mazie Bridges?

Castle Reign's firewalls that protected the identity of the players were impressive, but Holden had been hacking electronic security systems since they'd come into existence. One of the few advantages of having lived for as long as he had was that he'd had plenty of time to learn plenty of things. He wasn't truly immortal in that he could be killed, but he'd stopped aging when his gargoyle form had stopped evolving.

So, Knight Fury now played at Baker Street. That was interesting, but not overly surprising. She was a gentle soul, although she had the heart of a warrior. It would certainly explain why she hadn't been online as much lately. He'd been gladdened to see that she still planned to meet him and the others at the Coal Hole at eight tomorrow.

He tried to suppress a wry grin. He wondered what their reactions might be to one another. Rook was a stunning blonde whose avatar looked like a yeti on steroids. Bishop was the quintessential computer nerd—barely old enough to drink, tall, lanky, and his avatar resembled a cartoonish Viking Raider with long, flowing locks and a full beard.

When he'd discovered a picture of Mazie, she

looked nothing at all like he thought she'd look. She wasn't as tall as he'd imagined, but he figured she'd fit under his arm easily. She had a curvaceous figure—soft and enticing. She kept her short dark hair in a flattering cut—not long enough to fist, but he could do without that. Her avatar looked like it had been based on Rook—a tall blonde with a lean, well-toned body. Holden realized regardless of her avatar, he'd have recognized her anywhere.

His own avatar was a tall, muscular figure who wore black breeches and a black shirt, with a high-necked cape that turned into wings. The face resembled a plague mask. He was known as ruthless, relentless, and dangerous.

When he entered the lounge, he discovered Adam was right—Mazie was curled up on one of the couches with several Doms surrounding her. She was bright and flirtatious. He'd noticed that same teasing and enticing manner had begun to enter her game play. It seemed Mazie was finding herself at Baker Street. The young Doms all seemed to be flitting around her like bees around a flower they wanted to pollinate. If anyone was going to be pollinating Mazie, it would be him.

Young? That pretty much included everyone in the club, as far as he knew. Holden hadn't spotted any vampires, although he did know several shifters played here. When you weren't exactly human, you tended to notice others who weren't either. For the most part they simply acknowledged each other's presence and went about their own business.

One of the unattached blonde submissives approached him. "Good evening, Master Holden. Are you looking for a partner tonight?" she asked hopefully, lowering her eyes.

She was lovely and he'd played with her before, but the only sub he had any interest in this evening was neither tall nor blonde, and it looked like he'd best make his move before someone else snatched her up.

"Thank you, Becky, but I see my intended prey is just over there," he said kindly.

"Lucky girl," said Becky, with no hard feelings.

Holden made his way toward Mazie. It seemed his interest had not gone unnoticed, and the entire bar seemed to go quiet as everyone watched him closing the distance to his prey. He knew there was music playing and people were whispering, but his entire focus was on her.

He'd only seen pictures of her in her frumpy street clothes, and she'd looked fine even without the proper clothing. But Mazie in a corset and boy shorts was a revelation that made his cock harden and strain against his leathers. Her boobs were pushed up, just barely contained by the corset, and her waist was nipped in nicely. And unlike a lot of women these days, she had hips that a man could hold onto and fuck her for days.

"Are you looking to play, Mazie?" Holden heard one of the younger Doms ask.

"If she is," Holden interrupted, "it won't be with you."

"Now see here, Tremayne," sputtered the young man, standing up as if to challenge him, but backing off at the penetrating glare he received for his trouble.

Holden turned away from him. "Tell him, Mazie. Tell him you already have a Dom for the evening," said Holden, ignoring the younger Dom. He extended his hand to her. "Come along, Mazie."

"I… I don't know you," she said but took his hand anyway, uncurling her legs and standing next to him.

Holden leaned down, running his hand down her spine to rest on the full swell of her ass. "Search inside yourself and you'll find me there."

Her hands came up to rest on his chest as she craned her neck to look up at him. Interesting. There was no innocent look there, but rather an interest and curiosity that matched his own. Holden folded his arms around her. For the first time in his very long existence, he wondered what it might be like to enfold Mazie within his wings to keep her safe and close to him. That thought came unbidden. Holden knew that for him that kind of closeness was impossible, because he could never be honest about who, or more importantly, what he was.

Holden could feel and see the uptick in her

arousal. Adam hadn't been wrong; Mazie Bridges was very responsive. She smiled up at him.

"I don't even know your name."

"Holden Tremayne at your service," he said, lifting one of her hands to his mouth and pressing his lips to her fingers. "Now, tell these little boys to go away. Tell them."

He dropped his voice down so low that it took on a kind, but commanding tone he felt Mazie would respond to. She never once took her eyes from his.

"Uhm, I guess my dance card is filled."

Holden suspected that if she even knew what a dance card was it was only because she'd read it in a romance novel.

Once again, he leaned down to whisper in her ear. "If I have my way, little one, that won't be the only thing that gets filled. Will you give over to me for the rest of the night?" She nodded. "Good girl. Let's go have a drink while I ask someone to set up a scene for us. Are you shy?"

She smiled and it was as if the light inside her could chase the darkest shadows from every corner of the room. "No. I thought I would be at first, but I find I have just a bit of an exhibitionist in me."

"Then we'll give them a show. By the time I make you come on stage, no one in the audience will escape our spell. And then I'll take you up to one of the private playrooms and take my time with you. You will serve me well this night."

Holden leaned down and swept her up into his arms, carrying her to a more dimly lit portion of the bar usually reserved for Doms with a sub needing aftercare, but Mazie was new to all of this, and he meant to give her a night she would never forget. Perhaps it would also light a fire for him that would shine brightly for years to come.

"Yes, Sir," she said, her eyes never leaving his.

∽

Mazie had never imagined anyone could lift her in his arms as if her weight was nothing. She'd learned in her training classes not to make comments like that at Baker Street. The second time she had, she'd been subjected to a nasty spanking by one of the resident Doms.

When he lowered himself into the chair, he arranged her so that she was sitting in his lap in such a way that she couldn't balance herself. As Holden arranged his arms around her, one hand resting on the inside of her thigh, Mazie figured it was deliberate. He motioned to one of the waitstaff. This was a man given to command. He wasn't just dominant in a club; he was pure alpha male and dominance was in his DNA. So, what the hell did he want with her?

"I wouldn't like what you're thinking, would I?" he said.

Knowing anything less than candid honesty could

get her into all kinds of trouble, Mazie opted for the truth as she settled against him. "No, Sir. I don't think you would."

When the staff person arrived, Holden said, "Do you know if the St. Andrew's Cross in the main room is available?"

"Yes, Sir, it is," was the answer.

"Good. Would you ask Adam to let me have it in about fifteen minutes and if someone could grab my kit and put it on the table, I'd appreciate it. Also, I'd like a whiskey neat. Bring Mazie a water."

"What if I'd like something stronger?"

"Alcohol dulls the senses and I want you to feel everything."

Something in the way he'd said that intrigued, aroused, and frightened her.

"Would you mind getting us an order of sweet potato crostini with prosciutto, goat cheese, and honey roasted figs?" When the waitstaff left, he said to her, "Do I make you nervous, little one?"

"Not really. I mean, I know this is a safe place and no one would let you hurt me, but I just met you and now I'm sitting in your lap with your cock throbbing beneath me and my boobs pushed up in your face. I'm new at this and I've never been bound to a St. Andrew's Cross… And I'm now blithering like an idiot."

"No. In your most charming way, you are letting me know how you feel. You're nervous and aroused—

just how I want you. Can you trust me to keep you safe and make this a memorable evening for you?"

She wasn't sure why, but when he asked her the question that way, all she could do was nod and say, "Yes, Sir."

"I know that Baker Street is your first club. You picked one of the best. I can tell you that most of the rest won't measure up. But you've been through the training class and understand the stoplight system, yes?" She nodded again. "How do you prefer to play?"

Play? What the hell did he mean by that? She knew that people referred to what went on in here as playing or scening, but… Oh, that. "I had all my health screenings, and I've now been on the pill long enough that I am one hundred percent bulletproof. No concerns there."

"I can use a condom if you like," he murmured, nuzzling her neck and allowing his finger to slip under the hem of her very, very short boy shorts.

Just a smidge more and he'd be stroking her very wet, very swollen sex. He traced abstract figures on the inside of her legs and across her mons. She could feel pressure building. One of the things Mazie had discovered in Baker Street was that she much preferred the touch of a man than that of a vibrator or her own hand. If he didn't stop soon, she was going to come all over his hand or at the very least her pussy was going to leak onto his very nice leathers.

"But if you do that, Sir, however will you fill me up?"

She thought for a moment she'd insulted him or been too bratty. Her training Dom had told her she'd best learn to embrace being spanked, as he thought it would happen on a frequent basis, especially if she was ever collared.

Instead of being angry or reprimanding her for her sassy comment, Holden Tremayne began to laugh. "Do you want me to fill you up, Mazie? Do you want to feel my cum as it bathes your pussy with its warmth?"

"Yes, Sir. I've never not used a condom, but something about the way you said it sounds like I've been missing out."

"Good. Because I would very much like to spill myself inside you… repeatedly."

The staff person brought their drinks and Holden fed her the crostini, which had to be one of the best things she'd ever eaten.

"This is delicious. Thank you."

"They rather remind me of oral sex. The prosciutto and goat cheese are tangy and salty like my cum, and the roasted fig is like the honey that is beginning to coat my fingers."

Holden continued to seduce and arouse her with voice, words, food, and touch—all coming together to form the most powerful aphrodisiac she'd ever experienced. She knew she wasn't going to get drunk since she was only drinking water, but Mazie found him to be far more intoxicating than any alcohol that had ever passed her lips.

Every time she managed to drag her eyes away from him, she could see that the two of them had become the center of attention. More than one Dom was holding his sub in a similar way, playing with her as both parties watched.

"Pay them no mind, Mazie. All those Doms are jealous of the beautiful woman I hold in my lap."

"And the subs are wishing it was your fingers." She gasped as just the tip of his finger penetrated her core to take some of her arousal and swirl it all around her clit without actually touching the little nub.

"Yes," he whispered. "But these fingers are only for you."

They finished the crostini and Holden swirled the last of his drink in the heavy crystal tumbler before swallowing it down. As he finished, he nuzzled her and removed his hand from her shorts. She felt the loss like a deep aching. There had been something decadent and wonderful about having him play with her while others watched, even though they really hadn't been able to see anything. When he stood, he hauled her up into his arms, cradled her close to his chest, and strode from the room onto the main floor of the dungeon.

He set her down facing the St. Andrew's cross.

The languidness she had experienced upstairs was gone in a heartbeat. Next to the cross was a tall side table; on it was a flogger and some kind of glove. She looked down and couldn't miss the way his hard length pressed against his fly. Well, at least she was having the same effect on him that he was on her.

She stared. She couldn't help it—it seemed to her as if their bodies were already synchronized. She watched his cock pulse beneath his leather pants and felt her pussy fall into harmonic rhythm with it. He was hard, she was soft. He would fill her in more ways than one and she could envelop his staff within her wet heat. Her pussy truly ached. She needed to feel him inside her, shoved in deeply before he began to stroke her to ecstasy. And she needed him to fill her with his cum. She couldn't imagine being denied that.

Holden helped her to step out of the boy shorts before pulling a knife from his boot, inserting the point underneath the bottom of her laces of her corset, and neatly pulling up and out to sever them as if they were made of spider's web. She was naked in front of a room full of people, and she didn't care. All that mattered was this magical connection with Holden.

"Where are you?" he said softly.

"Baker Street. Oh—green, Sir. I'm green."

Holden chuckled. "I'm going to take such good care of you, little one. Will you trust me to do that tonight?"

She nodded as he lifted first one arm and then the other to the top of each section of the cross. He ran his hand down her spine, so that she could feel his touch, and she allowed herself to sag into the piece of equipment as he bent down to bind her ankles. Now she was spreadeagled.

"Ready?" he whispered, removing his leather vest and grasping her throat with one hand as he nuzzled her neck and allowed his cock to rest against the crevice of her ass.

"Yes, Sir."

His hand left her throat, to trace along the base of her neck until he ran it down her back, gently squeezing each of her ass cheeks.

"I'm going to spank you someday—for discipline, pleasure or both." Mazie's body trembled. It was almost as if she could not only feel it but see it. Wherever he touched, goosebumps followed in the wake of his fingers. "I think my little one finds the idea of submitting to me on a deeper level enticing."

Out of the corner of her eye, she saw him step back to the side table and pick up a black flogger with seven falls. He shook it loose and swung it back and forth, letting the falls come alive.

Holden stepped back, lifted the flogger, and then swung his arm down, the first strike hitting her ass and the back of her thighs with a gentle *thud*. There was a bit of discomfort, but that soon gave way to the most incredible warmth. It spread from where the falls had landed and radiated outward to encompass her entire body. Mazie moaned, not from pain but from a pleasure bordering on ecstasy.

The flogger rose and fell in a rhythm that encouraged her to embrace his control and mastery over the instrument and of her. He struck her major muscle groups—back, thighs, and buttocks, allowing more gentle strikes to wrap over her shoulders and flick her breasts and nipples. A thin veil of a dreamy kind of fog descended. Any and all tension and fear leached away as Holden worked her over.

When Holden finally allowed the flogger to drop by his side, he came close to her and rubbed his hands all over her back and buttocks, ensuring he'd done no damage. He slipped his hand between her thighs and played with her pussy, and Mazie came with the startled cry of his name. Pure pleasure surged through her system.

He leaned in. "And now those Doms are cursing themselves for being so foolish as to not challenge me for you. But do not fear, little one, I would have won, for you are a prize worth having. More?"

"Please, Sir."

CHAPTER 5

Holden resumed his place and nodded to someone she couldn't see. Pulsing Celtic music filled the air. He picked up a second flogger and began to wield it slowly, rhythmically. He made a figure-eight pattern along her back, which Mazie remembered when turned on its side was the symbol for infinity. The floggers fell on her naked flesh in time with the music and Mazie could feel herself dropping deeper and deeper into what she was sure was subspace. Desire reignited and began to spread through her body like wildfire. It was an interesting contrast—her mind and soul were set free while her body and arousal were bound to the cross and to this man.

Everything that came next—each strike of the falls, each beat of the music—filled her with a distinctive passion that caused her to shiver and tremble in response. As she could feel her body racing toward another orgasm, it all stopped. There was no flogger, no music. She was bereft at the loss.

"Fear not, little one. You said you trusted me."

"I do, Sir."

"Good girl," he rumbled seductively, allowing the sound to wash over her body and make her quiver.

He picked up what looked to be a black velvet glove with a heavy nap—it had to be some kind of vampire glove. Holden ran the glove across the tops of her shoulders, down her chest, and over each breast, pushing the small spikes through the material so that they scored her nipples. She went over the edge of the abyss into another climax.

"Better," he murmured, and ran the glove all over her back in a zigzag pattern.

Mazie moaned and arched her back into the soft material, preening until the slight bite of the metal stubs raked across her naked flesh. Again and again, Holden stroked her with the glove, eliciting her response until she shuddered, biting back another moan as she softly came. The rounded tips of the metal retreated into the glove until all that she could feel was the silk velvet as he stroked her, allowing her to float back to earth.

"You are extraordinary. You handled that wonderfully," he said. With one hand on her and the other wielding his knife, he cut her free.

Her knees buckled and she would have fallen had

it not been for Holden's strong arms catching her as she sagged. He lifted her in his arms once more. Where had this man been all her life? Would she ever experience this connection with him again?

"I'll take care of this," said Adam as he handed Holden a soft, cashmere blanket, which he managed to wrap around her without putting her down. "Room three is free if you want it."

"We're not done, are we little one?"

"No, Sir."

Holden left the dungeon area and carried her to the main staircase where he jogged gently up the steps and strode down the hall to one of the private playrooms. The door was slightly ajar, and he nudged it open with the back of his shoulder so that he could enter with her and kick the door closed behind them. He removed the blanket and laid her down on the turned-back bed.

He sat on the edge of the mattress and pulled off his boots. When she tried to sit up, Holden pushed her back down, pressing her into the mattress and pinched the nipple closest to him, giving a sharp tweak that went straight to her pussy. He stood, unlacing the fly of his leathers. The loss of his touch and his nearness made all her usual worries and fears come racing back to the fore.

Downstairs, bound naked to a St. Andrew's Cross in a room full of people, she had felt confident, beautiful, and at peace. Now, alone with him, her doubts began to creep back in. Holden Tremayne was gorgeous. His back was strong and sculpted with muscles that rippled when he moved. When he turned around, it was all she could do not to drool, and any question she had about whether or not he found her attractive was put to rest when she saw the size and rigidity of his enormous cock. He was like a perfect sculpture with broad shoulders, a cut chest, and six-pack abs chiseled out of stone. His gorgeous torso flowed into powerful thighs and long legs. Looking down, she could see even his feet were sexy.

There was also something intriguing about him. For all his physical perfection, there were raised wheals all along his back from his shoulders to his hips. At first glance they seemed to mar his sheer beauty, but the more she looked at them, the more she wanted to reach out and touch this imperfection that seemed only to reflect just how beautiful the rest of him was. Mazie wondered how they'd come to be. Had they hurt? Did he despise them?

"Did you doubt what you do to me?" he growled.

"Not really. I mean I could feel a connection downstairs, but…"

"Was that during the first or second time you came for me?"

She could feel a blush creeping onto her face as she knelt on the bed before him. He looked down at her, his cock weeping precum, and he stared at her. He stroked his cock once before both hands reached to take hold of her breasts, squeezing them gently and skimming down to her waist before allowing them to flow to her hips.

"You have the most luscious body. You were built to provide a man with an inordinate amount of pleasure for hours at a stretch. And you will give me those hours. Tonight, I'm going to put you on your knees and fuck you from behind so I can enjoy you."

Mazie felt her body shiver from the sound of his words and intensity of his gaze. Her nipples tightened into even harder nubs and her areolas seemed to darken. He spun her around on her knees, forcing her onto all fours with one hand on the nape of her neck as the other reached up to slide his fingers through the petals of her sex until he found her little jewel. Her pussy was weeping freely, and she groaned when he pinched her clit. She gushed her arousal, coating his hands.

He chuckled. "I hope you don't have anything strenuous planned for tomorrow, little one. I'm going to fuck you so hard."

She'd never known words could affect her the way his did. Her entire body shivered, still thrumming with the passion he had elicited from her when he had her bound to the cross. She responded to Holden on a primal level she'd never experienced before. Somehow her body and soul had known this was her natural mate. She knew he needed to complete their connection, and he needed to do it now.

The hand on the nape of her neck stroked down her spine, and he grasped her hips. The head of his cock probed between her legs and Mazie groaned. He let go of her hip and used one hand to guide his cock to her entrance before returning it to her hip. The swollen head began to part her labia, began to breach her, and Mazie cried out from the rapturous feeling. He had a monster of a cock and it had been so long since she'd been with a man. She hadn't had intercourse with her training partner, wanting to save that for a special occasion. She knew without a doubt this was transformative and she knew being with Holden was what she'd been waiting for.

The pressure began as his cock breached her opening and found its way inside. He pressed up inside her, working carefully so he wouldn't hurt her, but Mazie knew there was no way that would happen. She was so wet and soft and ready for him. He thrust in part way and then pulled back, only to surge forward again. He repeated the motion again and again, each time getting a little deeper and each time her pussy fought to keep him inside.

"Please, Sir," she pleaded.

"When you have trouble walking in the morning, don't say I didn't warn you."

Holden tightened his grip and thrust hard and deep, forcing another climax from her as she called his name. Arousal spiked, combining with pressure, tension, and pure hedonistic pleasure. He filled her completely and then some. She wanted to push back, to move with him, but Holden held her still. He stroked within her powerfully with increasing speed. He fucked her roughly and possessively as if he wanted to brand her with the experience and make her his own. She thought she might die and just as he pushed her over the edge into the abyss of rapture, she cried out. He shoved himself deep, holding himself inside her, and shook as his cock pumped her full of his cum.

Covering her with his body, he wrapped his arms around her and eased them both onto their sides, while still buried in her.

"Rest while you can, little one. I will have need of you again this night."

∽

Mazie slept, replete in his arms. She had exceeded any and all expectations he might have had. When he'd cracked her avatar to find out that Knight Fury was Mazie Bridges, he'd become obsessed with her. He'd studied how she played Castle Reign. He loved how her mind worked, how she was capable of great aggressive play combined with a subtlety and stealth that he greatly admired. He had worked to get Rook to propose the Phantom Guild and include Knight Fury in it. Neither Rook nor Bishop had wanted her. Knight Fury wasn't a flashy player. They had wanted to keep the group smaller—the fewer the members of the Guild, the larger their portions would be of the prize. He knew that although Rook hadn't met Bishop in real life, he did know they had discussed their strengths and even sent each other pictures. The fear was that without seeing Knight Fury, they feared that he or she might slow them down in the real world.

They were wrong. She might not be long and lean with a runner's body like Rook, but she was fit and strong. If push came to shove, he'd far prefer to have Mazie at his side.

He needed to find a way to tell Mazie who he was. He knew that the current balance of power between them was unfair. Unlike some so-called wannabe Doms, he had no problem taking control of any given situation and dominating a sub but knowing who she was outside of the club and what she liked to do when she wasn't at work gave him an unfair advantage. For him, the exchange needed to be equal, each party getting and receiving what they needed and wanted.

Holden knew he should tell her when she woke. Better yet, he should wake her and come clean. Wasn't that what D/s was all about? A Dom couldn't very well discipline his sub for lying or not being brutally honest if he wasn't doing the same. The problem was, he didn't want to risk losing her. It had been centuries since he'd last felt the kind of connection he felt with Mazie. No, that wasn't true. He'd never felt that kind of connection with any other being.

But he only had so much time before morning came and he would turn to stone. He'd always ensured he knew the exact time of each sunrise so he would have enough time to get back to his perch unseen. But no longer could he sense the dawn coming.

CHAPTER 6

Mazie woke in her own bed in Notting Hill. The morning light was soft as it filtered through the gossamer sheers that she used on her windows. She had blackout shades, but she rarely used them. Being at the top of a house that had no other buildings across from it meant no one could look in. Her room was small by most people's standards, but she loved it. She liked to think of it as a mini studio, as it did have its own kitchenette, washer/dryer combo, and bath. She was something of a minimalist as far as belongings were concerned. Her most valuable possession was her computer system.

She vaguely recalled Holden Tremayne bringing her home. They'd made love… No, she told herself, not made love, had sex—great sex—twice more. By the time he carried her into the bath and bathed her in the shower, she had left subspace, but her body was well aware of the excesses it had been subjected to when bound to the St. Andrew's Cross and later in bed with Holden. Groaning, she pulled the covers back and swung her legs over the edge of the mattress. She glanced down and realized she was naked.

The actual memory of Holden bringing her to her room made desire bloom. He'd been amazing—romantic, dominant, caring—everything she could have asked for in her first full-on D/s relationship.

"I was careful with the floggers," he'd said. "There shouldn't be any lasting marks or discomfort."

"And afterward? I'm pretty sure you and that lethal weapon you keep between your legs might have a lot to apologize for."

He'd chuckled. "How should I make it up to you little one?"

"Another time?"

She hoped she hadn't sounded needy or clingy, even though she felt both. That was a first for her since she'd joined the club. Her interactions so far had been enjoyable, but nothing compared to what she'd experienced with Holden. But then, he was the first Dom she'd had sex with. He'd been commanding and dominant, exacting from her precisely what he wanted each time he reached for her, at the same time ensuring that she had been pleasured in a way she'd never even imagined.

"I am at your disposal, little one."

"I'm busy tonight, I'm meeting some gamer friends. Did I tell you I play online video games? I could do the night after, though… I mean, if you like."

"I would very much like that, but fair warning, if you disappoint me and fail to show at the club, when I find you—and I will—there will be discipline."

"I would never willingly disappoint you," she'd said.

"Then we shall get along well. Why don't we meet in the lounge at, say, seven?"

She'd nodded and Holden had drawn her into his embrace and kissed her, pressing his lips to hers, his tongue foraging deep and dancing with hers. Winding her arms around his neck and letting him pull her close had felt as natural and normal as anything in her life.

After a leisurely exploration of her mouth, he'd kissed her hand again. "Sleep well, little one. I look forward to seeing you Thursday."

She'd closed and locked her door and drifted off to bed and to sleep.

After she got out of bed, she made herself a cup of espresso, her espresso machine being another one of her indulgences. She grabbed two frozen waffles and put them in the toaster while she nuked a couple of sausage patties. Not the best breakfast, but certainly not the worst.

Mazie opened the large chifforobe that contained

all of her clothes. She almost wished she had to be at work, but alas, she was supposed to attend a luncheon with her mother and sisters. Cinderella had nothing on Mazie, even if she wasn't a stepchild. Her eldest sister was getting married, and her mother and sister were beginning the planning. Mazie had tried to demur to being a member of the wedding party, but her mother had insisted and what her mother wanted, her mother usually got.

But she was also meeting with Rook, Bishop and Silent Knight, the enigmatic leader of their guild. Rook had been the one to approach her about forming an alliance to participate in Castle Reign's real-life quest, but Mazie was fairly sure her inclusion had been at Silent Knight's suggestion. They had come to each other's aid several times inside the online game over the past year, so it made some sense.

It was funny to think about all the good that had come out of her gaining membership at Baker Street. She was certain if her family knew what it was, they'd have a collective meltdown. In some dreamy fantasy she'd had as they headed to her place last night, Holden had wanted to stay and had agreed to come as her plus one to her sister's wedding. But that was a fantasy. Her reality was almost as good though, as he wanted to play with her again.

Since she would most likely be going to the Coal Hole directly from her meeting with her family, Mazie opted for a pair of black knit leggings, a red and black paisley top, a chic black jacket, and a pair of black ankle booties. If she had time, she wanted to see if she couldn't find some more stylish things to add to her wardrobe. She was sorry she hadn't taken Anne Watson's offer to help her with that. Mazie had to admit, she'd done wonders for Corinne.

She grabbed the waffles out of the toaster, slathered them with butter, and then sandwiched the two sausage patties between them. She sat down at her small round kitchen table. She only had two chairs, but then she didn't really entertain. Looking around, she couldn't help but wonder if Holden hadn't wanted to stay once he saw where and how she lived. Her place was at the top of a rowhouse in the fashionable Notting Hill neighborhood but wasn't much bigger than the private playroom they'd shared at Baker Street.

She shook her head and reminded herself that he had wanted to play with her again so she couldn't have been that big of a disappointment. Oh man, if the Doms at Baker Street could hear what went on inside her head, especially away from the club, she'd never sit down again.

Once she added make-up and fluffed her hair, she headed out. She kept a small Vespa scooter in a corner of the rowhouse's garden.

Walking it out into the alley behind the rowhouse, she made sure the garden gate was closed, put on her helmet, and then hopped on and started it up, stowing her small purse in the compartment behind her seat. There were those at the Savoy who thought she was nuts riding a scooter in London's notoriously awful traffic, but it didn't bother her. The scooter was small, but its relatively powerful engine got her where she wanted to go and could generally be maneuvered in and out of traffic with ease.

Her first stop was a shop Corinne had suggested to her. The salesclerk was incredibly helpful, and Mazie spent more than she should have, arranging for her purchases to be delivered to her at the Savoy. She didn't need to join her family at lunch with a lot of clothing bags. They'd want to see inside them, which would lead to a discussion about their cost, which would lead to talking about why she didn't move out of her tiny little flat. The fact was, she liked her tiny little flat and she was saving up for the day she might be able to buy a studio flat like the one Corinne had just bought from Rachel Holmes.

Mazie made her way to the restaurant on the edge of Soho and was glad to see that they had parking available. She removed the helmet, exchanging it for her handbag, and then headed into the restaurant.

"Mazie! Mazie!" her mother called, as if Mazie might not be able to spot them.

Sitting with her mother were her two sisters, her aunt and her cousin. *Oh swell. I'm going to need more than a pint when I get to the Coal Hole this evening.*

Mazie joined them, sitting on the end of the

booth seat next to her aunt, who gave her leg a squeeze under the table. Mazie picked up the cocktail menu, flipping it over to see what they had on tap.

Taking the menu away from her, her aunt said, "We ordered a bottle of wine. We'll get them to bring another glass."

There was a time when Mazie might have just acquiesced and sipped on the wine, but if it had done nothing else, her training at Baker Street had taught her to speak her mind and to get what she wanted.

"Thanks, Aunt Ellen, but I really don't care for wine." Mazie picked up the menu with the beer and ales on tap. "Ooh, they have Otter Ale on tap."

When the waitress came over to bring the wine and some appetizers, Mazie requested her ale and then picked up the food menu. They had shepherd's pie, which she loved, and it was supposed to be very good here.

"We're all having cobb salads, dear," her mother said pointedly.

Mazie's sisters were both tall and beautiful. They resembled her mother with their stylish blonde hair, slender bodies, and long legs. Mazie, on the other hand, resembled her father's side of the family, specifically her paternal grandmother—short and stocky with black hair… and the most amazing leftover buzz from the time she'd spent with Holden the night before.

She handed the waitress her menu. "I'd like the

shepherd's pie, and can I get a cup of the lobster bisque soup instead of the side salad?"

The waitress was built more like Mazie than those at the table with her. She smiled in recognition and understanding. "Since there's six of you, I'll get another basket of rolls and butter."

"Mazie," said her sister Eugenie, "I do hope you'll watch your weight after we get the bridesmaid's dresses ordered. You'd hate to have to pay to have it let out."

"Not to worry," answered Mazie, popping a bite of the excellent yeast roll in her mouth. "I pretty much stay the same size and I have no intention of ordering a dress one size too small and hoping I can diet my way into it."

"You really are impossible," said her sister. "With that attitude, it's no wonder you can't catch a man."

"I can't catch a man, dear sister, probably because I'm not out hunting one."

Mazie let her mind drift back to the night before and all the things she'd discovered about herself during her exploration of the D/s lifestyle. It had been a shock to her as to just how submissive she was. What had been an even bigger surprise was how peaceful it made her feel. There were some things in the lifestyle that scared and intrigued her at the same time.

Her mother, officious as ever, got out her large

planner. "I'm assuming that as usual, you will be attending solo."

"Not necessarily. I spent the evening with a really nice guy…" and she realized for all his hunkiness and gorgeous physique, Holden really was a nice guy. "Depending on how things play out, I might like to invite him. I know the venue will need a final head count a few days before and I promise to let you know by then."

Mazie's family let that pass and began discussing wedding plans. She had to wonder why she'd been invited to the lunch in the first place. It was obvious that none of them cared about or wanted her opinion. It must be that all the bridesmaids had to attend all these little gatherings and because she was Eugenie's sister, she had to be included as a member of the bridal party. She downed the last of her ale and when the waitress brought their meal, she ordered another.

Lunch lasted an interminably long time, and by the time it was finished, Mazie was ready for the whole day to be done. They'd picked the restaurant because of its close proximity to the bridal shop. The wedding had been put on a fast track, and Mazie suspected her eldest sister was pregnant but chose to keep her thoughts to herself. Eugenie could only look at dresses that were in stock, but as she looked like a model there were a number of them to pick from.

Once they'd settled on a dress for the bride, it was time to look at bridesmaid dresses. Eugenie's colors were a blushing pink and navy blue. The men were to wear navy blue tuxes, which meant the bridesmaids would be wearing pink. It wasn't the worst color on Mazie, but it was damn close. And the style… well, at least they were floor length. They'd looked good on her sister and cousin, but hideous on Mazie, which hadn't bothered anyone but Mazie. She decided she'd wear the gown during the ceremony and for the official pictures, but she would take something to change into once her official duties were done.

Finally, at the end of the day, Mazie's mother announced everyone was coming back to the house for dinner.

"I'm sorry, Mom, I have plans," said Mazie.

"You what? Since when? We still have things to discuss," said her mother in mild outrage.

"You never said this little get-together would last into the evening. I have plans I can't change."

"I don't care. This is your sister's wedding, and it takes precedence."

"Maybe in your and Eugenie's life, but not in mine. If you would let me have some notice, I could try to plan around when I'm needed, but that isn't the case today and I'm not willing to ask my friends to postpone our dinner."

That was another thing D/s had taught her—even if you weren't the one with the most power in a situation, you still had a right to set boundaries and expect people to respect them.

"I insist," hissed her mother quietly.

"No," said Mazie.

Her mother, aunt, Eugenie, and her cousin huffed off. Her other sister grinned at her. "Way to grow a spine, Mazie."

Taking a deep breath, Mazie headed back to the restaurant where they'd had lunch and picked up her scooter. Realizing she had enough time to do so, she headed back to Notting Hill.

CHAPTER 7

The sun had set, and the moon had begun its graceful ascension into the night sky. Sentience dawned a few minutes before the stone began to crack and fall away. It had taken some time for him to learn not to panic and to trust that he wouldn't suffocate in those few moments between awareness and being free. Sometimes he wondered if an even worse curse would have been to be fully aware during the time he slept in his granite tomb.

Holden climbed down from his perch. What the hell was he going to do about Mazie? His cock throbbed, reminding him he needed to figure something out and he needed to do it now. If she walked into the Coal Hole and realized he was Silent Knight, she might very well accuse him of lying to her, and rightly so. She might decide he had violated her trust to the point it could not be regained. It wasn't something he was willing to risk.

He pulled on a pair of jeans and boots, stuffing a white shirt, his laptop, and his mobile into a messenger bag. Ensuring no one could see him, he called forth his wings and glided down to the street below, retracting them and donning his shirt. He jogged to the tube station and took it to his favorite all-night coffee shop. He would beg off for tonight and then contact Mazie later and start trying to lay the groundwork to make things right with her.

His cock reminded him that he needed to figure it out—sooner rather than later. His cock was sometimes smarter than he was but rarely understood the subtleties of real life. He needed her to need him, to want to be with him. He knew she was new to the lifestyle, and he doubted that she had a lot of real-world experience with sex. The chemistry and combustion between them last night had been incendiary. He could use that. He could use sex to bring her close and make her need him.

Holden wasn't a fool, and neither was Mazie. He smiled. It was probably best if he was buried balls-deep in Mazie when he told her the truth. He could pin her to the bed and make her listen to him—he'd give her no other choice. But between now and then, if he could keep her, Rook, and Bishop at bay, he would build a relationship with her, one grounded in the reality of what they had and could have. After all, he was the Dom, and she was his sub. That was probably something he ought to do as well—get her collared or at least under a contract before he told her. Then she'd have to listen, wouldn't she?

There was also the matter of having been cursed back in the Thirteenth Century and that he was a stone gargoyle by day and a man with some gargoyle *accessories* by night. No big deal, right?

He hopped onto Castle Reign's game chat.

SilentKnight: Any of you there?

Rook: Just me.

SilentKnight: I'm not going to be able to make it. I was involved in an MVA and got banged up. No broken bones or lasting damage, but I'm pretty much stuck at home for the next two weeks.

If he worked it right, two weeks ought to be enough for him to bring Mazie close enough that she could forgive his lying about being in an accident. As for the whole gargoyle thing, well he'd figure out how to handle that when the time came.

SilentKnight: I'm kind of out of it tonight, but I can do chats while I'm laid up.

Rook: I'm sorry to hear that. Are you sure you don't need anything? I can be a wonderful nurse when I try.

SilentKnight: I'll bet you can be anything you put your mind to, but you guys can do the preliminary work tonight. We need to get registered to play. In order to do that, we have to pay the fee and fill out the paperwork. I'll take care of paying the fee so all you have to do is fill out the paperwork. They'll need a designated contact; I think Knight Fury would be the best person for that.

Rook:Okay, but we'll miss you. Are you close to a computer if we need to ask you anything?

SilentKnight:Yes. Also, ask the others if they're comfortable giving each other our email addresses in case we want to connect outside of the game. It might make it quicker and more efficient.

Rook:Will do. Are you sure you don't need anything?

SilentKnight:No, I'm fine, Rook. Thanks.

End of Chat

At least he'd bought himself some time. Not much, but perhaps enough. Mazie's response to him the night before was what had always been missing from his life. It hadn't been that difficult being a gargoyle, as he tended to be solitary by nature. Places and ways to find anonymous sex had always been around. It wasn't until he'd discovered BDSM that he'd begun to explore what made him tick sexually, and then he looked deeper into himself.

Baker Street had become a place of solace and service for him. As odd as it might have sounded to those outside the lifestyle, being a Dom—at least the way he and most of the Doms at Baker Street saw it

—was all about service. Many subs needed domination as much as he needed their submission. It was a give-and-take proposition—an honest exchange where both parties got their needs met.

Holden didn't try to fool himself by believing that providing dominance to a sexual partner was his way into the light and the end to his curse. But what would ending the curse mean? Would he become a normal, mortal man who no longer turned into a stone monster by day? Would he lose his wings, the only part of being a gargoyle that followed him into his human form? He would miss his wings. The ability to have them present at times and not at others had proven useful in more than one circumstance. And he loved the feeling of flight. Flying high above the streets of London and gliding among the clouds had often been the only time, outside of sex, that he found anything resembling peace or joy.

He put away his musings and focused on the tasks at hand. He needed to go into Castle Reign and pay the fee for the Phantom Guild to play its ARG in real life. He also wanted to double-check the date and time that the quest would begin. The quest was a kind of scavenger hunt for the pieces of a treasure map. Once the map was assembled, players would have to follow it to the final location where they would seize the prize—a magickal orb that they could exchange for half a million dollars. The rules for the real life ARG specifically prohibited bullying, intimidation, cheating, and violence. Anyone violating the rules would be booted from the game and if needed, reported to the police.

Only after teams or individuals had registered and paid their fee, would the first clue to the game be released to all the players. After that, how far and how fast they retrieved the pieces of the treasure map was up to them. Only after the computer confirmed that all pieces to the map had been collected and their trinkets contained within the geocache, would players be given the key code for entry into the final location. It was still up to players to find the location, but at least they could get in once they got there.

All in all, the quest had been well thought out and Holden was convinced the game's creators had gone to great lengths to see that it was fun and interesting and to minimize anyone's ability to cheat. The quest was also designed to support the MMORPG. They had also made the prize generous enough so as to entice even the purest of online only players to come out from behind their computer screens and into the real world… or at least partner up with one or more people in order to win.

Game chat exclusive to the real life ARG was allowed and one of the advantages of forming an alliance was that alliance members could set up a private chat room, exclusive only to them so that they could converse in real time. They could download an app to their mobiles that could be used as a scanner to aid in their quests. All relevant clues would be found sequentially but finding clues with the scanner meant that they received additional helpful hints. Holden was sure that downloading the app gave those behind the game some kind of useful information. He didn't care.

Holden had determined he would win the monetary prize, but he meant to win the other two prizes: Mazie and a way back to his humanity.

Mazie returned to the rowhouse and parked her scooter. She really didn't like driving it after dark. And the later it got, the more likely some of her fellow drivers would be inebriated. She freshened up and then headed for the Tube. The distance between Notting Hill and the Strand was just a hop, skip, and a jump via London's underground system. Arriving at the Coal Hole, Mazie asked a passing staff member for the location of the Phantom Guild's table. The guy grinned and pointed to a booth in a back corner. Only two of the other three guild members were present. She knew instinctively that neither of them was Silent Knight. She knew people's avatars rarely resembled them in real life, but somehow, she just couldn't conceive of either of them having the mysteriously creepy and sexy avatar of Silent Knight. The thin, nerdy-looking geek with glasses and a prominent Adam's apple just had to be Bishop, which meant, if she was right, that the tall, gorgeous blonde had to be Rook. The funny part was that Mazie's avatar looked as though she'd based it on Rook.

Mazie crossed the room, and the blonde stood, which only emphasized how beautiful she was. "I'm Rook, and this is Bishop. You must be Knight Fury—I love the name, by the way."

"How do you know I'm not Silent Knight?" asked Mazie.

"Because he—at least I'm assuming he's a he—messaged me earlier saying he'd been involved in a motor vehicle accident and was kind of out of commission, so for the next couple of weeks he's only available in the chat room."

Mazie sat down and ordered a Diet Coke with ice. When the others looked at her questioningly, she explained, "I had lunch with my family earlier today and had two Otter Ales, so no more alcohol for me." Bishop shrugged and took a drink of his pint.

"I love Otter Ale!" said Rook. Mazie figured that was one point in her favor.

"If Silent Knight is going to be laid up, I don't think we should wait to get started," said Mazie. "There's an awful lot of online chatter within the game and in social media. I'm not saying we exclude him, but maybe he can just participate virtually."

"Agreed," said Rook.

"Do you and Silent Knight know each other outside of the game?" asked Bishop.

"No, why?" responded Rook.

"He's probably thinking my avatar looks a lot like you do in real life and nothing like your avatar in the game," said Mazie with a grin.

"Yeah, well, not to be conceited, but it's nice to be appreciated for my brain and gamesmanship instead of my boobs," Rook said with a bitter laugh, and then passed it off with a wave of her hand. "I know I shouldn't complain, but sometimes it's hard to never be seen as anything other than blonde hair and big tits."

Mazie had thought she might not like the stunning beauty, but she realized Rook was probably right and that in the game, she could be whoever she wanted.

"How'd you come up with your avatar?" Bishop asked Mazie.

"Complete opposite of Rook. I wanted to be noticed for my looks." They all laughed. "And you?"

"I wanted him to be all I wasn't, although I do have some Viking blood in my DNA," answered Bishop. "So that leads us to wondering about Silent Knight. What's with the plague mask?"

"What if it's not a mask, but rather a reflection of how he sees himself?" offered Rook.

"That's too deep for me," said Mazie, lightening the moment. "So, what's everybody having?"

"You're the one who suggested this place," said

Rook, looking around the room. "It's very cool. But is the food good?"

"It's fairly close to my work and is a favorite of all of my coworkers. I can honestly say I've never had anything bad here and have never heard anyone say they didn't like the food."

"So, what are you having?" asked Bishop.

"I'm going to have the steak and pale ale pie."

"I was thinking about the vegan lentil cottage pie," said Rook.

Mazie nodded. "I'm not vegan, but I've had it. It was delicious."

"I feel like something different. How's the Buttermilk Chicken Burger?"

"Fabulous. I love burgers in general, but if I'm here and wanting a burger or a sandwich, that's my go-to," said Mazie, pleased with herself that they all seemed to like the place she'd suggested.

I am such a sub… such a people pleaser.

They ordered their food and while they waited, Rook said, "I have to tell you, I wasn't going to try for this thing. I knew I couldn't do it alone and didn't feel like I knew anyone well enough to ask. And to be perfectly honest, it was Silent Knight who suggested the Guild and its members."

"Same here," said Bishop. "I mean about not doing it. But when Rook messaged me and told me who was in it, I looked up our rankings. Talk about a hit to the ego. I'm the lowest-ranked member."

"I don't know that being ranked eighth overall in a game whose online subscriptions have reached more than five million is a bad thing," said Rook.

"True enough, but you're ranked fifth, and Knight Fury is second…" said Bishop.

"I am? Last time I checked I was fourth, but close to taking over third," said Mazie.

Bishop laughed. "That maneuver you pulled off when you stole that guy's mojo bag and got him to take out the evil swordsman for you was brilliant. That bumped you up to second, and of course, Silent Knight is the perpetual leader."

"I checked everybody's rankings too," said Rook, making Mazie feel as if she'd somehow been lax in not checking them out as well. "When I chatted with Silent Knight earlier, he said the game wants any alliances to have a single contact person and he suggested Knight Fury. I looked into it and other than getting us registered, it doesn't look like it would take up too much time and I am not the most organized."

Bishop laughed. "And I tend to be anal. I'd drive you guys nuts."

Mazie felt herself relaxing and really beginning to like her other guild members. "That's no problem, I can do that. I was wondering on the way over here, if we might want to exchange email addresses, even if it's just one you want to set up specifically for this."

"Great minds," said Rook. "Silent Knight suggested the same thing."

Both she and Bishop agreed. They jotted down their emails in her phone. "I'll check with Silent Knight and get his. Then I'll set up a group email and distribute them to everybody."

They finished their meal, and all agreed to meet online not the following night, but the one after.

As they were heading out the door, Mazie said, "We're supposed to get the first clue upon payment of the entry, but no one is to start the quest until one minute after midnight next Saturday. But as soon as I have the clue, I'll attach it to the group email."

They agreed to keep in touch and to meet back in person on the Friday before the game was to start, if not before. Each headed off in a different direction. Above, a silent sentry stood watching.

CHAPTER 8

The next week had flown by. Mazie had spent almost every night at the club with Holden. They alternated between watching others, just relaxing together in the lounge, and becoming one of the favorites for others to watch. She'd lost any and all self-consciousness she'd had about being in various stages of undress or being observed by others. She no longer cared what others thought. As long as she pleased Holden and felt her needs were being seen to, the rest of the world could go hang.

Holden was an exciting, creative, and experienced Dom. He always seemed to know just what she wanted and what would give her the best experience. He most often had her in his lap if they were watching others scene or when they were up in the lounge. But there were times he directed her to the floor to sit between his thighs. She'd learned about teasing or trying to entice him when he said no.

∽

Her head rested on his thigh, but every so often she rubbed the spot where his cock strained to get out. At first he'd thought she was having trouble getting comfortable. Then when it kept happening, he realized she was deliberately provoking him, trying to get him to take her upstairs. She'd been aroused from the moment she'd sat down; he could scent her delicate sweetness and took pride and joy in the fact that she would be ready for him long before he touched her.

Holden fisted the hair at the crown of her head, lifting her head from where it rested against the inside of his leg. "Having fun?" he growled.

"Not as much as I could if you'd finish your scotch and take me upstairs," she said cheekily.

"Now why would I do that?"

"Because you're hard and I'm wet."

He leaned over, running his hand down her naked lower body and between her legs, parting her labia and slipping his fingers up inside her while he pressed his thumb against her clit. Mazie's startled gasp became a low moan.

"Why yes you are. But as I recall, you got your bottom spanked the other night for playing with me without permission. Apparently, the lesson didn't take.

So, we'll try something different. Unlace my leathers and take my cock out."

"Here? In the lounge?"

"And be quick about it, unless you'd prefer to get spanked before you do it so that your pretty red ass is on display." He waited. "Now, Mazie."

She was quick to obey. Not because she was afraid of him, but because she was deeply submissive and wanted to please him. He'd spent the better part of an evening teaching her precisely the way he wanted her to suck his dick, and she enjoyed practicing. So did he. He loved fucking Mazie, but he also enjoyed having her go down on him and also going down on her.

Her hands went quickly to his laces, freeing his desperately hard cock. Mazie licked her lips. She was going to enjoy this and so was he. Mazie's tongue came out to lick his staff from its base all the way to the head. She circled her tongue around and then licked back down to his balls, which were already heavy and tight. Gently she reached up to cup them as she whispered kisses on them.

Holden was practicing every bit of self-control he had. As much as he loved the feel of her mouth on him, nothing compared to sinking into her and stroking her until she was writhing beneath him, calling his name as her pussy convulsed all along his cock. God, he loved that.

She swiped her tongue back up to the head and licked up the first drop of precum before sucking his staff into her mouth. She sucked his cock as if it were her favorite lollipop, using deep, rhythmic sucking interspersed with long passes of her tongue. Arousal and need surged throughout his system, threatening to unleash the primal beast that laid within.

He lay his hand on her head, petting her as he watched her swallow him down. Holden groaned. No one had ever given him head the way that she did. There was no tit-for-tat, just Mazie's unadulterated pleasure in servicing him. Each time he groaned, she shivered, and he could scent her ever increasing desire. She would be more than ready when he got around to fucking her.

Mazie greedily suckled the head of his cock, suffusing heat throughout his system. Warmth flared and he groaned again as she laved her submission and affection all over his cock. He realized he had become a possessive asshole. He wanted a collar on her, wanted others to know with just a look that she was private property—not that he worried about where her affections lay.

The familiar tingle at the base of his spine warned him that he was about to go off like a cannon. He held her head and began to move, pumping his hips back and forth. Her teeth just barely grazed along his skin. Finally, he shoved himself all the way to the back of her throat, unleashing a torrent of cum and sending it straight down into her belly. Mazie kept sucking until she'd gotten every last drop.

He knew others were watching, knew they were getting off on how she sucked him off, but what they didn't understand was the joy with which she did it. When he let go in her, whether in her pussy or her mouth—they hadn't had the anal discussion yet—he did so in pure bliss, connected to her in a way he hadn't been to anyone in his life.

When he finished, he stroked her short, spiky hair, leaned down to kiss her forehead, and whispered, "Now, carefully put my cock back in my leathers, lace me up and think about the fact that it's going to be a while before you get anything." She started to protest, and he placed his finger over her lips, shaking his head.

～

It was a lesson well learned. Holden was something of an indulgent Dom and yet he pushed her limits. He seemed to know her better than she oftentimes knew herself. Mazie found that in addition to impact play, she was inordinately fond of sensation play—vampire glove, Wartenberg wheel, and wax play had all fed into her hedonistic enjoyment of the way Holden topped her. She was still afraid of fire play, and he had been overly understanding and respectful of that.

He had added to her self-confidence in every aspect of her life. Her mother was annoyed that she was no longer always immediately available, willing to drop everything to come running or cancel plans because they'd forgotten to ask her if it was convenient for her. Her family had long ago decided that as she wasn't married, they could make plans convenient for them and that she'd just fall into line.

Mazie smiled and hugged herself as she headed out for Sunday brunch with Bishop and Rook. Silent Knight was still incapacitated but had checked in regularly. The first quest clue had set teams up to either participate in the game or not. The first geocache would contain the key that would open all the others. The clue read: *Dr. Jekyll's turned his face from the Stanhope Gate. Captured by the weapons from the First Great War, the vanquished beast sees no more.* It was crucial that they get this first clue right—if they failed to get the key within the first ninety-six hours of the game, they would be eliminated.

KnightFury:I received the clue and emailed it out to the group. Did everyone get it?

The other three sent a thumbs up emoji

Knight Fury:OK.

Rook:Clueless. Hyde Park isn't normally on my radar.

Bishop:First Great War is World War I

SilentKnight:Or the war to end all wars

KnightFury:Jekyll's turned face has to be Hyde so Hyde Park, but the rest eludes me

SilentKnight: The major weapons were gas, guns, and tanks. You can't capture gas and the tanks never left Europe, so it has to be guns.

KnightFury: The Cavalry Memorial—it was made from melted-down guns and the conquered and captured dragon is dead so sees never more.

Rook: That's bloody brilliant!

Bishop: The park opens at five in the morning. Knight Fury do you know where the memorial is located?

KnightFury: Yes. It's on Serpentine Road in the park by the bandstand. I have to go to work that day, but I can pick it up. Have we decided on our trinket?

Rook: I like the idea of the four-leaf clover since there are four of us

Bishop: I think we should either go with something that represents chess or a knight of armor or riding, or something to remind people we have two top players in our alliance

KnightFury: How about all three? There is a chess piece that is called the knight and it's represented by the head and neck of a war horse.

SilentKnight: I like that idea. Small, easily recognizable and a symbol of strength and versatility

Rook: I do ceramics and have some chess piece molds. I could do enough of them for our trinkets—we need nine, right?

Bishop: Yes. That would be great.

SilentKnight: I hate to be a wet blanket, but I

don't think any of us should go alone to any of these geocaches. There's a half a million at stake, and we all know gamers who would be willing to hurt somebody to win so let's agree—nobody travels alone. [thumbs up all around] OK.

End of Chat

∽

At five o'clock that Saturday morning, before the moon had set and the sun risen, fifteen teams were waiting at Stanhope Gate when the park opened. Mazie thought it would be a foot race and was surprised when all the others, including Bishop, seemed to start randomly searching. Mazie took him by the hand and led him quietly away.

"The clue said Stanhope Gate. I don't see any cavalry memorial," said Bishop.

Mazie nodded. "And originally that's where it was. But then it was moved to its current location, over by the bandstand."

They managed to slip away and were the first to find the geocache and put their trinket in, which triggered a device that revealed their cache key.

"Come on, let's go out a different gate so no one sees us," said Bishop.

"That's sneaky, Bishop. I like it."

Holding hands, they ran in a different direction from where the other teams still searched.

~

Holden was cutting it close. He knew he was. Sunrise would be upon him any moment, but he wanted to make sure she was safe. He had soared overhead, allowing the wind to rustle along his wingspan as he flew in the darkness, avoiding the silvery lunar path that cut through the clouds.

He watched as she and Bishop joined hands. His always present gargoyle essence rose up much closer to the surface this close to sunrise. The urge to swoop down and sweep her up in his arms and kill Bishop was difficult to resist, but now that he saw she was safe, he needed to get to Westminster Cathedral.

He soared up to this usual place along the tower and barely had time to settle onto his perch before the sun began to crawl over the horizon, its first rays reaching him as his stone sarcophagus began to enclose him. A sarcophagus, not a coffin. For like the pharaohs, he would rise again.

~

Later that evening, she met Bishop and Rook at the Coal Hole, an upscale pub, where they quickly ordered dinner. The game had acknowledged that they were in the lead, as theirs had been the first trinket put in the geocache.

"It was great," said Bishop. "The other teams were looking around and Knight Fury just grabbed my hand and led me straight there."

"Yeah, but it was your idea to go out a different gate so as to not give it away."

"When does the next clue drop?" asked Rook.

"Not until the other teams have been eliminated," said Bishop. "Then how fast a team goes is solely dependent on how quickly they solve the clues."

Mazie nodded. "Ninety-six hours to find the first clue seems really generous."

"Yes and no," said Rook. "I heard in the general chat area that there are more than a hundred teams playing."

"I'm surprised it's that few," said Mazie.

Rook took a long drink of her Otter Ale before speaking again. "Did you see the buy-in? Over a thousand bucks per team. Most players don't have that kind of money. I'd be hard-pressed to come up with a quarter of that amount. And if there are too many people on your team, it hardly seems worth it."

"While I think it's generous Silent Knight paid our buy-in, I think we should pay him back," said Mazie.

"While I agree in principle, it would be difficult. How about if he takes it out of the prize money?" said Rook.

"What if we don't win?" asked Bishop.

"Never happen," said Mazie and Rook in unison.

They finished dinner and agreed to talk in their private chat room as soon as the next clue arrived. Mazie wasn't seeing Holden that evening, which made her body ache with need, but he'd been adamant that she needed to rest.

CHAPTER 9

Holden watched them go their separate ways but followed Mazie to the Tube. She didn't seem to be overly concerned or in a hurry to get back to her place and seemed to wander in the general direction she wanted to go. He assumed she had come via the underground system, as he hadn't spotted her little scooter anywhere. He rolled his eyes. He knew it was practical, but the damn thing really wasn't safe in London traffic, especially after dark. It seemed as though she knew that too, and had opted to take the Tube, which was, in his opinion, much safer than the scooter. He was tempted to meet her at her place and invite her for a drink or a coffee, but he didn't want to seem overeager, even though he could never remember wanting a woman the way he wanted Mazie.

Over and over as his wings beat through the air, it

was as if he could hear them repeat the same old strain: *Go to her. Go to her. Go to her*. But with that would come the need for explanations that he was not yet ready to give. Last night had been spectacular, but even as inexperienced as she was, he knew she was sufficiently involved to submit completely and accept his explanations. He would bend her to his will, make her accept him as her Dom, and then figure out the rest.

He soared through the night sky—too restless to want to go to the coffee shop. Maybe Mazie would want to contact him through the game. Originally, he'd meant to follow her home to ensure she got there safely but decided that a 'chance' meeting in the Tube might offer him an opportunity to take her someplace to talk. As she window shopped along the Strand, Holden found a place to land and throw on his shirt before heading to the Tube station to beat her there.

Once he'd made sure she was headed for the same station, he jogged down the steps, bought an evening paper, and took up a casual lookout post. If he worked this right, she might spot him and approach him on her own. If not, he would approach her. Holden grinned. If he played this right, he might be able to find a way to spank her for not approaching him. That might just be the ticket.

Holden enjoyed disciplining a woman. There was something about the feel of a soft ass under his hand and watching it change from ivory to red that did things for him. He recognized that the vanilla world would tell him he was all kinds of perverted, but he knew differently. And even if he was a pervert, Mazie was perverted as well. While she and the other guild members had been having dinner, Holden had been able to call Baker Street and talk to Adam, who had given him an overview of Mazie's likes and dislikes, as well as her hard and soft limits.

"You know, you really should have gone over this with her that first night," Adam had said.

Even though he knew Adam had a point, he'd responded a bit testily. "Nothing we did that night was outside of Mazie's comfort zone, and she trusted me enough to see her home. I would think by now you would know me well enough to know that I am careful with my subs."

"You're right, but still. You should go over these things if you intend to sign a contract with her. I did read that right, didn't I?" he'd said.

"You did indeed, and I will take care of that before we play again tomorrow night. May I reserve the number three privacy suite at, say, about eight thirty?"

Adam had laughed. "Wow. I never thought I'd live to see the day the mighty Holden Tremayne got snatched up by a cute little button of a sub."

"She is more than a 'cute little button,'" Holden had responded. "She's smart, sweet, sensual, and one of the most beautiful subs that has ever graced Baker Street."

"I don't disagree. And certainly, I wouldn't disagree with a Dom's assessment of his sub… She is yours, isn't she?"

"Just as soon as I can convince her to say yes."

Adam had laughed again. "Another one bites the dust. We can get a contract done pretty quickly after you give us the specifics."

"I should have them tomorrow," Holden had assured him, hoping he wasn't wrong. The fact was that they had talked quite a bit last night as he'd held her close. Their likes and dislikes dovetailed nicely. Holden couldn't see where there would be any conflict.

As he stood on the platform waiting for her, he replayed the conversation with Adam in his head again. What troubled him wasn't whether or not Mazie would agree—he felt fairly confident about that. What he was trying to figure out was the ethics of having her agree to an exclusive contract if she didn't know all she really needed to know about him. But then, he reasoned, she could always nullify or cancel the contract. Yes, better to have a contract signed and in place first. One more thing to bind her to him.

The station was a hustle and bustle of activity, even at this time of night. It maybe wasn't as bad as during the commuter rush, but still there were a significant number of people around. He watched people come and go but found now that his eyes were drawn to couples and not to single, attractive females. It seemed he'd finally settled on the one female he was willing to risk everything for. If she didn't reciprocate his feelings, or if she chose to tell his secrets… No, he wouldn't contemplate that. Even if she couldn't forgive him for not being honest with her from the start, she would never betray him. He'd just have to pick up and find a new place to be alone.

He looked up to see her coming down the stairs. He liked the way she seemed to be aware of her surroundings, even when searching in her purse for her card. He dropped his head as if he were reading something of interest in his newspaper.

She walked up quietly beside him. "Holden? Am I allowed to approach you outside of the club?"

He lowered the paper and let his eyes sweep over her in lustful appraisal. It had to be lustful as his cock was pressed up hard against his fly. "I was sort of hoping you wouldn't."

Her face fell and an embarrassing stain began to creep up her cheeks. "I'm sorry."

Holden tossed the newspaper into the rubbish bin and hauled her into his arms. "I was hoping you wouldn't, little one, so I'd have an excuse to slap your pretty ass tomorrow night."

He could literally feel her entire body refill itself with confidence. He had to remember that she hadn't known him, or been in the lifestyle long enough, to know when he was teasing or to make an educated guess that Doms like him tended to find excuses to spank the asses of their sassy subs.

"I don't think I'd want that."

"Maybe not, but you'd enjoy it, and get all kinds of aroused. I hope you don't think my not spending the night with you has anything to do with you. It's about me and my schedule right now."

"Not at all, Sir," she purred. "I will admit, though, that I hope things will evolve and that perhaps we can spend more time than just the evenings together."

"I would very much like that. Are you headed home?"

"I was, unless I get a better offer."

She is going to make a spectacular brat.

"And how would you define better? I was headed for my favorite coffeehouse. I would love to have the pleasure of your…"

His words were cut off when a lanky teenager in a dark hoodie snatched Mazie's clutch bag. The perp rushed up the escalator.

"Stay here and get the transport police," he growled, handing her his messenger bag and charging after the guy.

Once the purse snatcher knew someone was in pursuit, he slipped up the side of the moving staircase, past people who were standing patiently. There was a large divider between the up and down escalators that had a shiny metal surface and was about two feet in width. The thief knew how to use the people on the escalator to his advantage, pushing through them and then pulling them back into place behind him to close up the hole as he slid along, hugging the median.

Holden kept his eyes on the kid as he attempted to escape. He was dressed nondescriptly—hoodie, jeans, dark T-shirt, and plain ball cap on his head. If he could put enough distance between them or get out onto the street, he could easily blend in and allow the city to swallow him up.

"Holden!" she cried. "Holden!"

He knew he should let the creep go, but he was damned if some asshole would steal Mazie's purse and get away with it. He turned to look at her as she made her way to the stairs.

"Stay there!" he shouted. "Stay and wait for the authorities. I'll be back for you."

"But I want to be with you," she yelled back.

"You'll bloody well do what I say. Damn it Mazie, obey me!"

He probably should have found a better way to say that, but he didn't have time to worry about the niceties of her learning to do as she was told. Lust fueled his adrenaline as he raced after the object of his pursuit. His need to retrieve her purse and play the hero was almost overwhelming.

The slimy bastard had recognized that Holden was gaining on him and leapt onto the median dividing the two staircases, somehow finding purchase with his sneakers as he ran up the steeply angled surface. The kid might be younger—*wasn't everyone?*—but Holden was stronger. He followed him onto the divider, gracefully beginning to make some headway in closing the distance between them.

He could hear shouting behind him, but he didn't pause to look. It wouldn't take long for the little creep to get to ground level and then he'd be gone. Holden forced himself to move forward, to keep his balance and to catch the kid. If he could just get a hand on him, even if he didn't immediately get her bag back, he could trip him up and send him sprawling.

The perp made another mistake as he looked back to see if Holden was still in pursuit. By being distracted from accomplishing his goal to get away, he gave Holden the opening he needed to push harder, forcing himself to put on a burst of speed as he reached out and grabbed the kid's hood, toppling him and sending him down the escalator.

Finding an opening in the throng on the moving stairs, Holden shouted, "Move!" as he landed and then turned to run down the staircase.

The teenager was dragging himself back to his feet. Realizing the only thing that might stop Holden was to lose the purse, the kid set it down on the median, careful to ensure it was easily seen before sprinting down the remainder of the escalator steps. Holden stopped long enough to retrieve Mazie's bag but feared that even that momentary loss of focus might allow his target to escape.

When he turned back to try and find the thief, he heard a gasp and then a thunderous round of applause. As he stepped off the escalator, he saw the cause of their approval. Sprawled on the ground with Mazie's knee in between his shoulder blades was the kid in the hoodie. He could hear people whispering about how she'd tripped him and then followed him down, pinning him until he couldn't move.

"Any chance you have handcuffs or a zip tie on you?" she asked, looking up innocently at him.

"I'm afraid not," he chuckled, just as members of the British Transport Police showed up to take over.

He held out his hand, offering it to Mazie. She took it, rose gracefully, and allowed the officers to take over in the apprehension of the teenager.

"You did quite well bringing this guy down," said one of the officers, who had moved them away from the thief. "Any reason he would have targeted you?"

"Why do you think Mazie was targeted?" asked Holden.

"Miss, would you mind showing me how you normally hold your purse?" asked the officer.

Mazie took her clutch bag, holding it close to her body with her entire forearm.

"See there? Your girl has a good hold of that bag, and it would be difficult to get it away from her. When you look at a lot of these gals, they are much easier targets with much bigger bags."

"I hadn't thought of that. Can you think of anything he might have wanted, sweetheart?"

"Nothing besides my cash and a couple of credit cards, and trust me, it wasn't worth stealing for any of that. I have my security ID for the Savoy, but unless he knew that's where I work, he wouldn't know to target me."

"Maybe he does know you work there," said the officer.

"No. I never wear my ID out and I work in security. I monitor the feeds all day; I'd have noticed him. I don't mean to sound like a snob but dressed like that he'd have stood out like a sore thumb."

"In that case, let me get your information and you can be on your way. We can take it from here."

They gave him the requested information and were allowed to leave.

"What kind of Dom are you? No handcuffs? No zip ties?" she teased.

"The kind that spanks naughty subs when they brat off at him," he replied, almost managing not to laugh.

"Promises, promises," she said, her eyes dancing as he directed her toward the platform where their train would soon be arriving.

CHAPTER 10

Taking her by the hand, he led her onto the train. The almost continually repeated warning to take care and watch the gap that existed between platform and train droned on. He ensured that she was safely on the train and escorted her toward the back. Seconds before they reached their seats, the doors closed with a whoosh of air and a bit of a jolt as the train pulled away from the platform. He handed her into the bench seat, next to the window.

"We make a good team, Sir," she said.

"We do, but I haven't yet decided whether or not I'm angry about you apprehending that thief."

"That thief," she laughed, "was a junkie teenager looking for an easy score." Mazie paused for a moment, as if considering her next words. "It occurs to me that you might not know that I trained to become a member of Scotland Yard."

He hadn't known that, but he very much liked that she was sharing it with him. "I didn't know that."

She nodded. "Yes, and I work in the Savoy's security department, heading up the cyber division of the security team. The kid didn't have a weapon and honestly, I must have outweighed him by a stone, if not two. He was never a danger to anyone but himself. But I'm sorry if it concerned you."

"I'll consider both your explanations and your apology," he said quietly. "Selfishly, I'm glad you don't work for the Yard, as I would be worried about you all the time. But they were fools not to hire you."

"Thank you. Gabriel Watson said the same thing to me when he hired me."

"You know Gabe and Anne?"

"Yes. I worked for Gabe when he was at the Savoy, and I was there when they fell in love and got married. I mean, we weren't super close friends, but I liked them both. They sponsored me and paid for my membership at Baker Street. Do you know them?"

Holden chuckled. "I know Gabe fairly well. We didn't really see each other outside of the club, but I think that had more to do with our schedules than anything else. Anne is a beauty and is so perfectly suited to Gabe. I actually feel sorry for the other Doms at Baker Street."

"Why is that?"

"They never had a shot at Sage, Rachel, Anne, Saoirse, or Corinne and now they've lost you as well."

"Have they?" she asked, searching his face.

"I would very much like it if they have."

"So would I," she said quietly.

They rode the rest of the way in a comfortable silence before he helped her out of her seat and off the train. They came up out of the Tube and walked the half block to the coffeehouse.

"Holden," called the barista. "Usual?"

"Yes," he said, then turned to Mazie. "And what would you like?"

"What are you having?"

"Usually at this time of night, I'm looking for something decadent. I tend to favor the toasted marshmallow latte."

"Too sweet." She scanned the menu. "How about Guinness-flavored espresso?"

"Bitter and sweet. We really do go together well, you and I. Care for anything to eat?"

"Those blueberry muffins look good."

"They are, but I like the orange cranberry scones better. Let's get one of each and we'll split them."

"Sounds good."

After giving the barista their full order, Holden escorted her to a comfy couch in the back with a low, long table in front of them, and then went back for their order, setting everything on the table in front of them before sitting down next to her. He made sure to sit so close that their legs were touching.

"So good," she purred, taking a sip of espresso.

"I'll have to remember you like it dark."

She looked him directly in the eye, grinned and quipped, "I'll take it any way you want to serve it."

Oh, she is in quite the mood.

"Yes, you will, but never forget you have safewords and I expect you to use them. Why don't you tell me what you did with your day?" he asked.

"I had lunch with my family again. I think I told you my older sister is getting married. But you'd be proud of me, when we were eating, my mother announced that she and my sister had planned something for all the bridesmaids to do and just dumped it on me to plan at the last minute. But I politely declined and then went ahead and did what I had planned."

He could feel the grin splitting his face. "You're right, I am proud of you. Were you with them all day?"

"Most of the day, but I had planned to meet again with my guild members in that game, and I didn't want to renege on them. I told you about that, right? Castle Reign's real-life quest?"

"You did."

"You probably think it's silly," she said, looking into her espresso, "but until I joined the club and met you, that's how I spent most of my time off. I'm ranked very highly in the game, and our guild was the first to solve the initial clue and get the key. Rumor has it there may be some sort of advantage down the road. Apparently, a lot of people missed the deadline and have been eliminated already. Odds are getting better for us to win." She sat up a little straighter and let out a little gasp. "Listen to me going on and on."

"Not at all. I can tell you enjoy it; it doesn't hurt anyone and is probably a lot safer than catching thieves in the underground."

She laughed. Holden realized he was quickly becoming addicted to the sound of her laughter. He hadn't had a lot of laughter in his life since he'd begun his lonely penance. Was Mazie an indication that the old ones were taking notice that he'd become a different kind of man? If the curse were really lifted, what would that mean for him? For him and Mazie?

"Did I tell you that the ARG quest has a prize of half a million US dollars? Our guild seems to work really well together. Our leader is sidelined but I've met with the others twice at the Coal Hole."

"Over on the Strand?" he asked, and she nodded. "Do you think your leader might just be letting the three of you do all the work and then they'll just step in to claim a quarter of the prize?" He held his breath, hoping she wouldn't express any annoyance at having been stood up by the fourth member—namely, him.

"No, not at all. Silent Knight—that's the name of

his avatar—conferences in and is incredibly intelligent."

"Silent Knight… Interesting name," said Holden.

"We all have avatars with made-up names."

"I don't think you've shared yours with me. Would you?"

"Knight Fury. It's a play on the name of a character I like in an animated movie. And Silent Knight contacted one of the other members to let her know he'd—well, we assume he's a he—was in an automobile accident and is laid up for a couple of weeks. That's why he's been gone. But we've been working our way through the clues together since the first clue dropped. Only teams that left their trinket and collected their key within the first ninety-six hours were allowed to continue. After that, teams can move only as fast as they can solve clues. Right now, my guild is still in the lead. I'll bet you're already tired of hearing me go on and on about a stupid game."

Holden shook his head. "Not at all. Anything that interests and excites you is something I want to hear about, and a half a million US dollars is nothing to sneeze at. Tell me what you're going to do when you win it."

"We have a really good team, but we don't know that we'll win."

"Don't say that. You have to believe you can win." He let that sink in. "So, what would you do with your share of the prize?"

"I'd use it as a down payment on a studio flat here in London."

"Don't you like where you're living now?"

"I do, but it's tiny, and I'm hoping that down the road I'll have a relationship and maybe he'd want to move in together. I'd like something nicer, and I'd rather be paying a mortgage and not just laying out rent each month."

"What if I told you I wanted the same thing?" he asked.

"With me?" she squeaked.

Holden chuckled. "Yes, with you. Which brings me to why I was glad we ran into each other. I know it might seem fast, and you are under no obligation, nor do I want you to feel any pressure, but I feel something special with you, Mazie."

"I can't believe you said that. I feel the same way."

"I'd very much like it if you'd sign an exclusivity contract with me and accept a collar from me."

He didn't even know he'd been holding his breath again until she nodded happily and said, "Yes. I'd like that too… and I feel the same way."

∽

They spent the next two hours not really negotiating, but more just talking about what they wanted and liked versus what they didn't want and didn't like and how firm those limits were. Mazie giggled and blushed profusely when he told her that she was not allowed to masturbate and that he wanted her private areas kept devoid of hair.

"They went over that in class, saying a lot of Doms had specific grooming requirements. I mean, I trimmed that area up, but why bare?" she asked.

"Any number of reasons. For one thing, keeping you bare provides me with a better visual in terms of being able to see your pussy whenever I want. And it's a good way for me to remind you as your Dom that you will bend to your Master's desires. In addition to those two reasons, I also like knowing that even when we're out and away from the club there isn't much between me and getting my hands on and in you."

"Just your hands? I'll be so disappointed."

"Keep bratting off on me and I'll tie you to the bed tomorrow night and keep you on the edge until I finally let you come, but still don't give you my cock."

Mazie closed her eyes and her entire body shivered. She liked it when he told her what he was going to do to her. He had the most wonderful deep voice. When he told her the things he wanted to do with her, it was incredibly erotic. She'd discovered that when he did them, it was even better. Holden had a way of saying some of the most perverted things—at least in other people's opinions—and making them sound loving and nurturing. If her Master was a deviant, then so was she.

When they got to her stop, Holden escorted Mazie

up to the street and they walked hand-in-hand toward the rowhouse where she lived. As they opened the gate to the front garden, the door to a black SUV opened up and DSI Michael Holmes stepped out.

"Holmes what are you doing here? Don't tell me the transit cops called a DSI about a purse snatching."

"What purse snatching?" Holmes asked, looking at Holden and doing a double take. "Holden Tremayne, isn't it?"

"DSI Holmes. It's good to see you again."

At first Mazie was confused and then she realized it shouldn't surprise her that the two Doms knew each other. After all, they were both members of Baker Street.

Holmes turned back to Mazie. "What purse snatching?"

"When we were coming home on the Tube, some skanky teenager tried to take my bag. Holden chased him while I called the authorities. We caught him, and they took him and our information and sent us on our way," explained Mazie.

"Mazie," said Holmes, taking her arm, "why don't you and I go up to your place. If I need anything from Mr. Tremayne, I can catch up with him later."

Holden shook his head, removed Holmes' hand from her, and stepped between her and Holmes. "We can go upstairs if you like, but Mazie is my sub."

"I don't see a collar."

"A fact that we plan to remedy tomorrow night. So, if you want to talk to her, you'll do it in my presence."

"You have no legal rights here, Tremayne. You're not her solicitor. Hell, you're not even her husband."

"All true, but unless you're arresting her, you have no legal right to prevent me from being by her side."

The two men were facing off, each sizing the other up. Testosterone could be toxic, she thought. "I tell you what, boys. If you want, you can just drop your trousers and I can decide which one looks bigger."

Both men shot her a startled look, then looked at each other and started to back down.

"Sorry, Tremayne. Mazie is someone I know. I promised Gabe I'd look out for her. If she's your sub, I suppose that responsibility now belongs to you."

"It does, but you had no way of knowing."

The two men shook hands.

"Does this mean I don't get to ogle both of your cocks?" she asked saucily.

Holden's hand connected sharply with her backside. "The only cock you need to worry about ogling is mine and if you aren't careful it's going to be a good long while before your next peek."

"You do know she's a crackerjack shot with both handguns and rifles, right?" asked Holmes. "But I digress. I think maybe all of us should go up to your place."

"Sure. Right this way," she said, leading them into the house and up the stairs to her flat.

When she opened the door and went to walk in, Holmes put up his arm to keep her from entering. He did so quietly, scanning the entire room, checking her chifforobe, under her bed and her bath.

"Holmes," said Mazie. "You're starting to scare me."

"Come on in here. Tremayne, can you shut the door please?"

Holden did as he asked and then drew her to the bed to sit down so they were facing Holmes.

"Mazie's right. The Yard didn't send a DSI out about a purse snatching."

"Are you sure everything that was in your purse before the guy nabbed it is still there?" asked Holmes.

Mazie opened the purse, taking each item out. "Yes, I'm sure. Everything is all here."

"What about in your wallet?" inquired Holden.

She checked her wallet. "Nothing missing. Even the first clue and the key are here in the compartment." She turned to Holmes. "I'm involved with an online real-life game quest. Holmes, you keep avoiding answering the question. Why are you here? It isn't about some junky teenager trying to snatch my purse, is it?"

Holmes took a deep breath, running his hand through his hair. "I'm afraid not. Do you know a guy named Elvis Sanders?"

Mazie shook her head. "No. I think I'd remember that name. Why?"

"What about you?" Holmes said, nodding his head toward Holden.

"Mazie isn't lying to you Holmes. She only knows Sanders by his avatar's name."

"What are you talking about?" she said looking at him.

"Elvis Sanders is Bishop."

How the hell did he know Bishop's real-life name? For that matter, how did he know the name of Bishop's avatar or that she knew him?

"How do you know all that?" she said, trying to pull her hand away.

Holden held fast. "I can explain, little one."

Mazie took her other hand and pushed his away. "I want explanations from both of you." Her voice sounded sharper than she'd meant it to. She was pretty damn sure Doms didn't take well to being snapped at, but at this precise moment, she didn't much give a damn.

"Holmes, why do you want to know about Bishop?" said Holden in an even tone.

"He's dead," said Holmes, watching Holden closely.

Mazie gasped and reached for Holden's hand and hers was enclosed immediately.

Holmes continued, "He took a header off a roof. I think they wanted it to look like suicide to the casual observer, but according to our forensics people, there's no way he could have landed where he did unless he was pushed, thrown, or had taken a huge running start and leaped. When we started looking, there were other indicators as well."

CHAPTER 11

Suddenly, Mazie felt light-headed. It didn't escape her notice that Holden had yet to answer her.

"So, you did know him," said Holmes, redirecting her attention to him.

"Uhm, yes. I didn't know his name, or at least not his real name. Can I see a picture?"

"I'll show you the one I have of his driver's license. You don't want to see his face after the fall."

Holmes held up his phone and showed her the driver's license. The man pictured was indeed the man she knew as Bishop.

"And he's in some online game with you?" asked Holmes.

"Yes, but right now we're also in an ARG—a real-life quest that's a component of the game."

"I understand that people can get a bit obsessive when playing these games."

Both Holden and Mazie laughed. "More than a bit," said Holden.

"The real-life quest has a prize of a half a million US. People from all over the globe have formed alliances and are teaming up. The game just got started, but already people are falling behind and dropping out."

"And you say your team is in the lead. Is there any way for people to know that?"

Holden nodded. "Yes. Both the online and real-life game keep a scoreboard so a player or alliance can always check their position in the game."

How the hell did Holden know all this? She wanted to believe, desperately, that Holden had researched the game because of her interest, but the roiling in the pit of her belly said that wasn't it at all.

"But how would someone know Bishop's real-life identity?" asked Mazie, looking pointedly at Holden.

"If you're talented enough, security systems' firewalls are more an annoyance than an obstacle," Holden answered.

Holmes looked at Holden and then back to Mazie. "You think this might be connected to this game?"

"I don't know that it is, but it makes some sense. A half a million isn't chump change."

"But why Bishop?" said Mazie. "I don't mean to

be unkind, but of the lot of us, he was the lowest ranked."

"If you think about it, it makes sense. They take out the lowest denominator and then work up from there. If you do it right, you might get one of the top competitors to join your alliance."

"How many are in your alliance?" asked Holmes.

"Four," answered Mazie. "Myself, Bishop, Rook, and Silent Knight. Although I guess Bishop is no longer a member of our alliance. I only know them by their avatar names. I have no idea who they are in real life. Maybe Mister Firewalls-Are-Annoying can answer that better than I."

"I wouldn't get snarky with me," said Holden.

"Do you know?" asked Holmes.

Holden nodded. "Obviously you know Mazie. Her avatar name is Knight Fury. The one she calls Rook is Samantha Butler."

"Wait a minute, Holmes, if you didn't know about the game and the avatar names, what brought you to my door?" asked Mazie.

"I found your mobile number in his wallet, as well as that of your friend Samantha. But this Silent Knight person is unaccounted for, and we can't seem to figure out who it is. And I'm not just talking about within the game. Whoever this person is, he's taken great pains to hide him or herself. I dispatched one of my officers to Ms. Butler's home and she'll be taken care of."

"There's more, isn't there?" asked Holden.

"I'm afraid so. But before we go into that, just who are you, Tremayne? I know all the stuff they have about you on file at Baker Street. I suspect the vast majority of it is fake, but I can't prove that; it's more a suspicion on my part and the fact that I think I recognize the signature of one of the best forgers in the world."

"So you know Nina. Impressive. She has managed to stay off most people's radar, especially the last couple of years. These 'other indicators' you mentioned, they've led you to believe the other members of the Phantom Guild are in danger, haven't they?"

Holmes nodded. "Yes. We found what we thought at first were tarot cards, but that now appear to be some kind of hand-made calling cards. There's something that looks like a one-eyed yeti on one of them."

"That would be Rook," said Mazie.

"And a Viking Warrior on another."

"Bishop."

"A gorgeous stacked and leggy blonde that resembled the woman you call Rook."

"Me. I'm known as Knight Fury."

"Forgive me, Mazie," said Holmes, "but you are neither tall nor blonde."

"What can I say? People treat the amazon goddess warriors better than the chubby girls with short hair."

Holmes smiled at Holden before continuing. "And

then a tall guy, all in black, with a cape, a hat, and a face only a mother could love."

"A plague mask," supplied Holden.

Mazie snatched her hand away. "Who are you?" she said, afraid she knew all too well.

Holmes looked at Holden, then Mazie. "The last figure, as I'm sure you have surmised, is Silent Knight."

"You're him, aren't you. You're Silent Knight. You've been lying to me. You've been lying all along. You lied to Rook and Bishop too. You were never involved in an MVA. God, how could I be so stupid!"

"That's enough, Mazie. You will not speak about yourself derogatorily. I can and will explain everything to you." He turned to Holmes. "I can stay with her tonight."

"Want to bet?" she said, fighting to hold back the tears.

Holmes looked at Holden. "My sub," said the latter quietly.

"The hell I am."

Ignoring her, he continued speaking to Holmes. "Mine."

Holmes smiled. "Yes, I saw the two of you together the other night. They can be a bit difficult at this stage."

Holden chuckled. "Fitzwallace told me JJ was a lot more manageable once he got a collar around her throat."

"Not happening," said Mazie, whose hurt was quickly being displaced by anger. How dare he lie to her.

"As I was saying before I was interrupted, I can stay with her tonight, but I have to be gone before sunrise. I don't think she should be here alone. I can call Fitz. They have a number of saferooms at Baker Street that she could use."

Holmes nodded. "Or we could put her up at my place or even at the Savoy."

"Hello! I'm sitting right here in the room." Mazie crossed her arms and could feel her face reddening with anger.

"Too far away from me, as far as I'm concerned. Why don't you come sit in my lap or on the floor between my legs," said Holden.

"Why don't you go fuck yourself?" she snarled.

"If you aren't very careful, little one, I'm going to forget we lost a friend tonight and put you over my knee for a discipline session."

"Bishop wasn't your friend. You never met him. God, he thought you walked on water. Wonder what he'd have done if he'd known you were lying to us all along."

"Mazie, I will give you that you have every right to be upset with me, but we will talk about this later. Holmes, I'm open to your suggestions as to where Mazie would be the safest."

"I think that would be the Savoy. We're putting

Ms. Butler up there as well. We know the hotel well and it would be more efficient to have them both there. That way Mazie can go to work if she wants."

"I don't want to stay at the hotel, and I can still bloody well do my job. I'm tired and I'm having a shitty day. So why don't you two sod off, and I'll go to bed," said Mazie, standing and walking to the door.

"The Savoy it is," said Holden. "Would you like to pack a bag, sweetheart, or would you like me to carry you?"

Mazie turned on Holmes. "You can't let him do this."

"A Dom never comes between another Dom and his sub."

"Fuck you," Mazie said in an even, deliberate tone. "Get out."

She opened the door and gestured for them to leave.

"Carry it is," said Holden. He stood and quickly covered the distance between them, tossing her over his broad shoulder as if she weighed no more than a stone or two. "Holmes, don't worry about getting her anything. The Savoy has robes and I'll pack a bag for her tomorrow."

"Put me down," she snarled.

"No," replied Holden.

When she wouldn't settle down, he smacked her ass several times, imparting a sting that had nothing to do with desire. He carried her down the stairs and back out to Holmes' SUV. Holmes opened the back door and Holden slipped them both in.

"This is kidnapping, you know," said Mazie. "I'm going to have you arrested and I'll have DSI Dickhead's badge."

"Mazie," said Holmes. "I understand you're upset. If Holden didn't tell you he was this Silent Knight, I'm sure you're feeling…"

"Don't you dare tell me how I'm feeling," she said angrily, managing to get herself on the other side of the SUV.

"Mazie, you are understandably angry with me, but DSI Holmes hasn't done anything."

"You don't get to tell me how to feel either," she growled.

"And with that, little one, you have crossed the line. I will deal with you when we get up to our room. Holmes, I think it might be better to go up to the back entrance and use the service elevator."

"I agree. I thought we might end up at the Savoy, so they're already holding a room. I have them on the same floor in rooms next to each other. We'll have two uniforms on the doors, two at the elevators, both on their floor and in the lobby."

"You seem quite concerned," said Holden.

"I am. What I didn't get a chance to say was that each of the tarot cards showed your avatars with their throats cut. We think Sanders was just the first victim.

We're working with the gaming company to get a list of names of the other teams."

"If they decide to be difficult, let me know. I can probably get them for you."

"What are you?" said Mazie. "Some malicious hacker? Is that why you have such weird hours? Geeze, Holmes, you must think I'm stupid. I'm having a kinky sex relationship with a guy I know virtually nothing about. Good thing the Yard didn't hire me."

Holmes shook his head. "They're so much fun when they keep digging that hole with righteous indignation, aren't they?"

"To be honest, I wouldn't know, although I am considering just how red her ass is going to be when I'm done. But Mazie will be my first collared sub."

"No, I won't."

"You agreed."

"You lied."

"You'll take my discipline and my collar, or safeword out." He let the threat hang there. "As I was saying, she will be my first sub to discipline as my own. As to your question, little one, I play the stock market with my own fortune. Right now, I've been doing rather well in gold futures. I only hack people's systems when I need information, and never information that will make me money. So, Holmes, you have someone?"

Holmes nodded. "A good friend named Eddy Chastain. They haven't invented a system Eddy can't hack. The Yard is trying to talk to him about heading up their Cyber Crime Unit."

They pulled into the service entrance of the Savoy.

"DSI Holmes," said a uniformed officer, "the other protectee is upstairs and they have the room ready for Ms. Bridges. The uniforms are in place."

"Good man," said Holmes, opening the back door.

Mazie scrambled out and ran to the cop. "DSI Holmes and this asshole with him are detaining me against my will."

The cop looked between her and Holmes.

Holden got out of the car, walked to her, taking her arm in a vice-like grip. Very quietly he said, "You are going to settle down and behave yourself or I am going to go sit down on those pallets, strip your pants down past your knees, flip that top up and blister your very fetching backside. My guess is most of these officers are nice vanilla types, but they'll probably also get a vicarious thrill by watching."

"I am not your sub, and you have no authority over me."

"Are you using your safeword?" he asked calmly.

"N-… no," she said, wondering why it was she couldn't bring herself to do it. Holden had known who she was all along, and he'd been lying to her about himself from the beginning. Yet she still couldn't say the word.

"Then you can either decide to behave and accompany me upstairs or push me just one more time, and get your bottom spanked before I haul you over my shoulder and take you upstairs."

When she said nothing, Holden caught her by the nape of her neck and tilted her head back, crushing his lips to hers. His other arm wrapped around her waist and hauled her close as his hand settled on her ass. There was no doubt what Holden had on his mind… how he meant to finish any discipline session he was inclined to inflict. His hard length throbbed against her belly as he captured her mouth and made a meal of it.

Mazie felt herself go compliant and surrender to him. Holden was pissed, concerned, and a bit desperate to reassert his dominance and have her accept it. Therein was the thing that called to her. He was alpha male, and yet he wanted her submission to be offered and his dominance willingly accepted.

She wanted to bite his bottom lip and spit her safeword in his face… but she couldn't. She found herself softening, leaning into his body and offering him everything he wanted.

She had so many questions, but they distilled down to only one. Why?

CHAPTER 12

They were escorted by two uniformed officers up to their room. When the door was opened the officers made a cursory check to ensure nothing of danger was there.

"Looks good. We've got a guard posted in the kitchen. If you want something, call down and ask for the officer. Everything in the mini bar has been brought in by us so it's safe."

"Don't you guys think you're going a little overboard? I know Bishop is dead and I'm sorry about that, but…"

"Thank you, officers. Mazie is a bit rattled by all that's happened. I'll see to her needs—all of them."

The uniforms left and Holden closed the door behind them, locking the night latch and making a far more thorough search of the room. It was one of the hotel's junior suites with a view of the River Thames. It didn't have two rooms, but it had a designated seating area as well as a sleeping one. She was sure the Savoy had extended the invitation to have her and Rook stay at the hotel as Mazie was an employee.

"And I thought they were paranoid."

"Not paranoid, little one, careful. Why don't you call Rook and make sure she's all right and then you and I are going to talk."

Mazie picked up her mobile and called Rook.

"Fury? What the hell? Did they tell you about Bishop?" said Rook, her voice breaking.

"Yes, I know people at the Yard. I've seen DSI Holmes in some tight jams, but I've never seen him rattled like this. Are you okay? Are you alone?"

"No, they have two guys outside and a very nice female officer here in the room with me. How about you?"

"I saw the guards outside, I'm right next door, and I have Silent Knight with me."

"Oh my God, is he all right?"

"No, he's a rat bastard and it seems I'm stuck with him, at least for tonight."

She looked at Holden whose glare told her he was not appreciative of her language or attitude. Well, he could opt out too. She was bloody well pissed at him, and he could just deal with it.

"What do you mean? Do you know him or something?"

"Or something. He's been my lover since shortly before the game started. He didn't deign to tell me that, or that he lied about the MVA. He's just fine. I've seen all his moving parts and they were all in working order—not sure that'll be the case come morning."

"This is the guy you were so gaga about?" asked Rook.

"Yes, well, apparently I'm a shitty judge of character."

"I'm sorry. How long are they going to keep us, do you know?"

"I'm not sure. I'll call a solicitor in the morning to find out our rights. I think you and I ought to finish the game."

"Absolutely not," growled Holden. "You and Rook are out of the game."

"Why not call her by her real name, lover? After all, you know it. See, he hacked the system and knew all of our real names. Samantha, by the way, I'm Mazie."

Samantha laughed a bit nervously. "It might take me a while. I got so used to calling you Fury. And I can't seem to think of Bishop as Elvis." Her voice was broken by a small sob. "He was such a sweet guy. Who would do this?"

"I don't know. And mad as I am at Holmes, if he's on the case, they won't get away with it."

She started to say more but Holden took away her

phone. "Samantha, I'm sure you're exhausted and emotionally spent. I know Mazie is. Why don't we all have breakfast in the morning? You're safe with all the security around here and Mazie and I are just next door."

"Is Mazie okay?"

"She's fine, just a little overwrought and more than righteously pissed off at me."

"Did you lie to her?"

"It was a lie of omission, but a lie nonetheless."

"Well, I agree with Fury. We're still going for the prize. The Yard can come along if they like. But we're going to win, and we'll send Bishop's share to any family he has."

"I think that's a lovely idea. I know both you and Mazie could use the money. But I think I'd like to offer up my share of the prize. That'll give you the money you need to leave your job and see if you can make it as a writer."

"How do you know about that?" she asked suspiciously.

"I make it my business to know with whom I'm playing."

"So, he cheats," called Mazie from across the room.

Holden sighed. "As I said, Mazie is a bit overwrought. She'll be better tomorrow. Why don't you go get some sleep and we'll see you in the morning? I need to get Mazie's things from her place tomorrow. Do you need anything from yours?"

"No, they let me pack some stuff and they're checking my computer tonight, so I'll have it back sometime tomorrow. Okay, then, I guess I'll see you in the morning. You be nice to Mazie and make things right with her, she's crazy about you."

"That's good to know. I may need you to remind her of that in the morning. I am madly in love with her, although she's not inclined to believe me at the moment."

"Whoa. Didn't see that coming," laughed Rook.

"Neither did I, but there it is. Try not to worry. You're in good hands. Sleep well."

He turned back toward Mazie. She had always disliked the term gobsmacked, but now she understood its true meaning and knew she was experiencing it. He loved her? Had he just told Rook he loved her? She shook herself mentally. No. That didn't matter. He had lied to her.

"Nothing to say to me?" he asked.

"If I answer that, it's something isn't it?"

Holden shook his head as he smiled. "If you've been wondering what it's like to have me truly pissed off and spank you, you're about to find out."

"You Neanderthal. D/s contracts aren't legally binding, and we've only talked about having one. We don't have one yet and you haven't given me a collar, so the way I see it, I'm still a free agent."

He laughed. "There's not a Dom at Baker Street who believes that. If you're not careful, I'll make sure the next time we're there we have a proper collaring ceremony and you'll only be allowed a corset, so your bright red tail is on display." He stopped, took a deep breath, and exhaled slowly. "I am trying to make allowances. Bishop was murdered and most likely by someone in the game, so there's a chance they're after you too. Added to that is the fact that I have been less than truthful with you."

"In the security business, we call that a lie."

"Enough, Mazie."

"I'm Fury to you."

"No, you are Mazie, my little one, my love."

"Bullshit."

"And that, little one, is a bridge too far," he said, advancing on her.

∽

Arousal, anger, and guilt were at war within him. He tamped the guilt down. There'd be time for that later. Lust pounded through him, feeding on what was bordering on rage. He was angry with her and himself, but his rage lay with whoever had killed poor Bishop and put him in the position in which he found himself now.

This was definitely not the way he'd planned to share this information with her. In fact, he wasn't sure there could have been a worse place or time, but he didn't have a choice now. He'd have to hope that he'd built a solid enough foundation that he could bring her back in line and get her to listen and to understand.

Adam had told him that she hadn't yet had enough time in the lifestyle to understand primal play. Maybe not, but she was about to find out that there were consequences to bratty behavior and some of it she wasn't going to like. When he got through with her, she wouldn't be sitting comfortably for a day or two.

Holden sat down on the edge of the bed, extending his hand to her. "Submit, Mazie. Now." She shook her head. "Are you safewording out?" Again she shook her head. "Decide, Mazie. Submit or safeword out."

Taking a deep breath, she walked over to him, pulled her pants down and put herself into position over his hard thigh. He closed his other leg behind hers but allowed her to rest the upper half of her body on the bed. Holden had to remind himself to keep breathing. She had the most spectacular ass and he'd wanted to spank it for a while. Oh, he'd given her a light spanking earlier in the week when they'd been playing, but he meant for this to be memorable.

He ran his hands over her rounded globes, caressing them then resting a hand on the small of her back. Holden brought his other hand up and back down in a short, sharp arc, resulting in a loud smack that reverberated all around them as Mazie hissed. Good, she needed to learn the difference right now between a playful or erotic spanking and a true discipline one.

So far, she'd learned how they connected when he played with her or made love to her. Now she would learn that connection came in all things, from emptying himself deep inside her to sipping coffee together. God, would he ever be able to share all that he was with her and have her accept that?

He spanked her with equal amounts of lust, love, and discipline. She hadn't experienced many spankings, so her backside colored easily. He rained his punishment for her language and her attitude. Yes, he hadn't been completely truthful with her, but he'd given her many chances to back down and behave. Holden covered her beautiful bottom and the backs of her thighs so that she squirmed and moaned.

Somewhere in the middle of his discipline, her gasp from the sting and heat morphed into a sweet moan of desire. That was what he was looking for. A couple more swats. He wanted her to wince when she went to sit in the morning. His entire body responded to her. His cock was hard as a rock and his body taut. He slowed the spanking until he could feel her writhing against his leg.

He stopped and caressed her ass again, enjoying the heat emanating from her flesh. He trailed his hand down and eased it between her relaxed and splayed thighs. He parted her labia and stroked her, finding her sex was swollen and wet. Slick with arousal, his little one was more than prepared for him. He rubbed the silky wet skin, taking some of her honey and rubbing it into her clit. He slipped a finger up inside her, curling it so he could stroke her sweet spot.

"Holden," she moaned.

A sharp, staccato slap to her backside. "What do you call me when we're playing?"

"Are we playing?" she snarked.

Her body might be ready, but she was still spoiling for a fight. That was fine, he still had hours to fuck her hard before he had to find his way to a roof and become the gargoyle once more. He smacked her ass another five times, ending with a single last swat to her pussy.

"Oh, Sir. I'm sorry."

"That's better. When I let you up off my knee, you're going to sit in my lap before I put you on your back and fuck you. I'm going to fuck you all night. I have to leave before the sun comes up, but if I hear about the Yard getting a repeat of your misbehavior, tomorrow's lesson will be given with a good, stout strap."

"Yes, Sir."

When he released her, he found no resistance in getting her to sit in his lap. At first, she was stiff and did her best not to squirm her sore bottom on his hard thigh.

"When you get punished, there is no comfortable way to sit, little one."

"You lied to me," she said, with more disappointment in her voice than anger.

"I know, and you deserve better than that from me. And there are still things you don't know. But none of it matters. You are my woman, my sub, my love. And you may expect better of me, but I also expect better of you. Your behavior tonight was less than exemplary."

She looked him in the eyes now, and he felt a softness in his heart he hadn't felt before. "I was hurt that you lied," she said.

"I know, little one, and I am so, so sorry. I didn't expect to find you, didn't expect to fall for you so fast and so hard. I thought I'd have time. I didn't plan to play with you that first night at Baker Street, and then I was in too deep. As I said, you deserve better. I don't want to hear from the officers that you were anything less than polite and cooperative. Do you understand me?"

"Yes, Sir."

Holden pressed his lips to hers. "Good girl."

He stood, lifting her in his arms as he did so. He set her on her feet, caging her within his embrace only long enough to pull the covers back and strip her naked. Holden dragged her against his body, slamming his mouth down on hers, plunging his tongue deep inside her mouth. He ran his hands down her back, reveling in the way she shivered and pressed herself closer. He cupped her blazing cheeks, squeezing and kneading them as she rubbed herself against his cock.

CHAPTER 13

*H*olden lifted her again, leaned over, and placed her gently on the bed. He tore at his own clothing, his usual control and elegance gone in the face of his need. Mazie realized in that instant that she didn't just need him, he needed her too. He stood at the end of the bed looking down at her.

"You are so incredibly beautiful. Spread your legs."

Mazie complied, enjoying her aching ass. It made her feel more submissive, more in tune with this man who watched her with naked lust and possessive passion. She was primed and ready for him, and she prayed he wouldn't make her wait and would simply fall on her, mounting her in one long hard push.

Holden lowered himself between her legs, taking his rightful place between them. His cock was hard and pointing to where it wanted to be. He reached under her to grab her ass and hold her as he shoved himself in. Her back arched in response as she cried out and orgasmed beneath him just from this simple act of possession.

He was enormous and he stretched her pussy every time he tunneled into her. She had come to understand that no matter how many times he took her, he would always claim her as his and his alone. He didn't move for the longest time as he looked down at her.

"Mine."

"Yes, Sir."

"Master. I'm your Master."

"Yes, Master."

"You'll bloody well take my collar and accept my authority."

"Yes, Master."

As her pussy softened and accepted him, he nodded and began to stroke. He pulled almost all the way out before slamming back in, which made her gasp. Her arms came up to wrap around him while her legs intertwined with his.

He groaned and growled as he pounded into her, taking what was his before he gave it all back to her. He hammered her pussy, his pelvis hitting her clit, making her dig her nails into his back as she cried out again. Her Master wanted to make sure she knew just which of them was dominant. As he thrust in and out of her with ruthless abandon, she had no doubt in her mind about who was who.

He continued to have at her, unleashing a feral part of himself she hadn't seen before, and that called to a corresponding place deep inside her. This was bliss, being locked in his embrace while he plunged in and out of her at a more furious pace. Her pussy quivered and trembled as she began to race toward ecstasy yet again. He wouldn't let up, building the pleasure until she screamed his name, her orgasm crashing down on her and threatening to drown her with its power and glory. One final, brutal thrust and Holden drove deep, grinding himself hard against her. He flooded her with his cum, his cock twitching and spurting out every last drop as she clung to him.

~

Holden smiled down at her. He could feel the dawn's approach. He'd never be able to make it back to Westminster Abbey before the sun cast its rays upon the city of London, which meant before he turned into a stone gargoyle. He would need to find a safe place to perch for the day. When he was the grotesque, he could sense nothing and was vulnerable to attack. Holden had learned over the centuries that when he was in his human form, he was almost impossible to kill. Wounds that would have left a regular human dead were healed during the course of the day while he was stone. But when he was stone? He could be destroyed by a well-aimed sledgehammer.

Mazie was sound asleep, dead to the world. She had stirred a bit when he eased himself out of bed but had settled back down when he'd stroked her hair and whispered soft words of love and sex. She was exhausted and would wake nursing a stinging backside and an aching pussy. Although given her responsive nature, he imagined she wouldn't mind the latter. Numerous times during the night, he'd taken her to the heights of pleasure, but also edged her to the point where her entire body had trembled with need.

She'd sworn at him, and he realized the time had come to get serious about being her Dom. After letting her sleep for an hour or so, he'd awakened her, spanked her again for language, and then taken her hard. And she had writhed beneath him, clinging to him and calling his name repeatedly.

Her hair was spikey and mussed, her lips swollen from his kisses and traces of beard burn from the dark stubble that usually adorned his face had marked her breasts, belly, and inner thighs. He had indulged his need for her throughout the course of the night, using her intensely. There was no question in his mind that he had found the one woman he'd been waiting for all his life, and he hadn't even known such a thing was possible.

Holden's system tingled and thrummed. The moon was setting, and he needed to go, or she'd find out the true extent of his lies to her. It bothered him that she still didn't know who and what he was or how he'd earned the terrible curse that had been laid upon him. He had long ago decided that it was unimportant as to whether or not he had actually fathered the child that had caused that poor girl to fall from the cliff, and the sea to claim her and the babe. What he had worked to reconcile himself with was that he had been cursed because of the arrogance and callousness of his youth. He had indulged himself in every way possible without a second thought to the havoc he might have caused. And now, even more than the curse itself, his past may well rob him of the one person, other than his sister, he had ever truly loved.

Pulling on his clothes, he slipped from their room, acknowledging the officers on duty. He made his way to the service elevator, but instead of going down the elevator to leave the building, he went up. He knew this area of London well. There was no place that a large granite gargoyle wouldn't be noticed. His only hope was that there was a place on the roof of the Savoy itself where he wouldn't be spotted. There were plenty of HVAC units, exhaust fans, ducts, communications equipment, and the like to afford him a secure place to hide both himself and his small bundle of personal items.

Holden could feel his limbs becoming heavy and knew he had to move fast. Finally, he located a spot where he would be difficult to see and that should afford him some safety until he would wake with the coming of the next night. He settled himself just in time as the stone began to encase him. For once he would welcome the oblivion of his daytime existence, for he wouldn't have to think about how he was going to tell Mazie about his curse and her most likely reaction. All he knew was that if she rejected him and told someone, they could go ahead and crush him into harmless pebbles because the idea of living without her filled him with sorrow.

∽

Mazie could feel the vestiges of sleep slipping away and instinctively tried to burrow against the warmth she always found in Holden's embrace. However, she found nothing other than room-temperature sheets with her fingers. As she left the last of her sleep behind, she vaguely remembered his telling her he had to leave. While that thought made her sad, the fact that Holden had told her he loved her was far and away the best feeling she'd ever known.

She rolled to her side and sat up, swinging her legs off the edge of the bed. *Youch! That hurt!* Her Dom and Master had definitely been in her bed last night, and according to her trashed backside he'd ensured she wouldn't be as given to acting out as she had last night. She got to her feet and went into the bath to get a robe. She turned away from the mirror and looked back over her shoulder. Her very red, swollen backside should have disgusted her or at least made her angry. Instead, it filled her with a warmth that was reassuring and erotic. *I'm one sick bitch*, she thought, laughing.

The hotel phone rang loudly, and Mazie rushed to answer it.

"You, Rook, and Silent Knight have been warned. Leave the game and the prize to those who deserve it," growled a malevolent voice before the line went dead.

Mazie ran to the hotel room door and flung it open.

"You all right, Miss?" asked one of the officers.

"Yes. No. Yes, I'm fine physically, but someone just called me on the hotel phone and threatened me."

"Please go back inside. We'll put out an alert."

"Would it be all right if Rook joined me?" she asked.

"The other protectee?" the officer asked. Mazie nodded. "I'll see if she's awake and would like to do that. Do not open this door to anyone but myself or Constable Smyth. Don't worry, Miss. We have you covered and you're safe. I'll have the Savoy send you up some breakfast. There'll be an officer in the kitchen to ensure the food is safe."

"Okay, thank you," Mazie said, returning to her room and locking the door.

A few minutes later there was a knock on the door

before Constable Smyth keyed in the lock code and opened the door, allowing Rook to come inside.

"Are you okay?" she asked. "The officer told me you got a threatening call. What the hell is going on?"

"I'm not sure what you mean," said Mazie, her mind still a bit befuddled from not having been awake for long, and the shock from someone trying to intimidate her.

"Half a million US is a lot of money, and I'm sure there are lots of unscrupulous people out there, even in the game, who would be willing to go to great lengths to win it. But murdering someone? Making a threatening phone call in a hotel full of uniformed police officers? That's a bit much, don't you think?"

Mazie went over to the in-room coffee/tea maker and made herself a cup of strong, black coffee. She held up an empty mug to offer the same to Rook, who shook her head and went to sit on the couch. "I hadn't really thought about it. I didn't get a lot of sleep last night."

"I'll bet," said Rook with a mischievous grin. "The female cop who stayed in my room said he was gorgeous. So Silent Knight is Holden Tremayne. That's really interesting."

"Yes, but why do you say that?" Mazie asked as she sat down on the settee, curling her legs underneath her.

"Whoa. Do you not know who Holden Tremayne is?"

"Not a clue."

"A very mysterious, uber wealthy investor. He manages his own fortune, which is said to be not inconsiderable, as well as the portfolios of a whole slew of very private and really wealthy men. He avoids publicity like the plague and the only known photos of him are grainy and from quite a distance away. He also is known to keep odd hours."

"He mentioned he trades stocks on exchanges all over the world so usually works at night."

Rook nodded. "That would coincide with what little is known about him."

"Holden knew who all three of us were before he agreed to join our alliance."

"That, too, makes sense, and I thought as much after I realized he'd manipulated me into forming the guild and inviting you, him, and Bishop into it. What doesn't make sense is why? It's not like he needs the money." She sighed and a sad look crossed her face. "So sad about Bishop. If the Yard hadn't figured out it was murder, I'd have made them listen."

"Why?"

"Simple," Rook said, rising from the couch and wandering over to the window to stare out at the Thames. "Bishop was afraid of heights. There's no way he would have gone close to the edge of a tall building."

Sipping her coffee, Mazie asked, "How do you know all this stuff?"

"I write romantic suspense novels, and I do lots of research for them. Sometimes that leads me down a rabbit hole, so I know lots of useless stuff."

"Sage Matthews writes paranormal romance and up until just recently she was a writer in residence here at the hotel."

"That makes it sound like you work here or have some affiliation with the Savoy," Rook said, turning from the view.

"I do. I work as part of the security team and head up the cyber security group, which makes my job sound far more important than it is."

"How fascinating. I'll bet you have a ton of stories to tell. Is Sage Matthews really as cool as I think she is? I'm a huge fan, and she's been a real inspiration to me," Rook said, crossing back over to the seating area.

"She's very, very nice and her husband is a brooding hunk. Don't get me wrong, I don't think Roark has ever said anything mean to anyone, but he can be very intimidating. He balances that with being dotty about Sage. So why do you think Holden brought us all together?"

"Probably because we're all smart—not just average intelligence, but more than that. I also think probably for specific skill sets. Like, I'm good at solving mysteries, you're good at electronics, Bishop was a highly regarded structural engineer, and probably Holden for his hacking skills."

"But what about Holden? I mean, I just thought

of it right this second. If he's got money, why's he doing it?"

"Probably to solve the puzzle or to win the game. I take it from last night's conversation that you had no idea that he was Silent Knight and that the two of you had become involved."

"Last night I was really pissed," Mazie said with a soft smile. "We met through another common interest and just connected in a major way. He seemed really sorry that he hadn't told me, and I suppose I can understand to a certain degree."

"Absolutely. That's a classic kind of misunderstanding. He probably didn't know, then didn't think it was important and then it was too late. So, the Yard is working on my laptop." Just then Rook's stomach growled, and Mazie laughed.

"I think I need some food. What do you say we have breakfast?"

"Sounds good."

Mazie called down and ordered a sampler so they could pick and choose. It wasn't on the menu or something room service normally provided, but she was part of the hotel's family, and they were happy to accommodate. It took their breakfast longer to reach them than it should have.

"Sorry, Mazie. The cop in the kitchen made the cooks open everything fresh. I guess they're worried someone would poison you guys?" said Ray, who was one of the regular waiters at the hotel.

Mazie rolled her eyes. "A guy we were in an online group with was murdered last night and the Yard seems to have gone a bit overboard."

"Ah, well, you can't be too careful then," Ray said. He set up their breakfast on the small dining table by the window and then left.

"You know, I was wondering why the Yard is so interested," said Rook, sitting down in front of her breakfast and starting to eat.

"Me too. It's a bit much. At first, I thought it was because I work here, and Holmes knows me. My guess is my old boss told him to watch out for me, but it just seems extreme."

"Yes. I can see them wanting us out of our homes as there was a direct threat, but putting us up at the Savoy?"

"That's definitely Holmes," said Mazie, moaning as she took her first bite of eggs benedict. "He was close friends with my boss and is good friends with Roark Samuels and Felix Spenser, who is the head of our concierge services, but the uniformed officers seem to me to be a bit over-the-top even for a guy like Holmes."

"I know! And without my laptop, I'm sort of lost with what to do with myself."

There was a knock on the door and Mazie dutifully checked the peephole to ensure it was a uniformed officer. Leaving the night latch on, she said, "ID please?" and the officer complied.

"I'm sorry to disturb you, but DSI Holmes asked one of the staff people here to go to your place and pack a bag for you, since you didn't have time to do it yourself," she said, handing the overnight bag to Mazie.

"Thanks," said Mazie as she took the bag and closed the door.

"They didn't give you time to pack? That seems rather rude," said Rook.

"Holmes did give me time, but I decided to use it to throw a major snit fit so Holden just hoisted me over his shoulder and took me out to the car."

"Oh swoon, I've always wanted to have someone do that, but I'm too tall."

"It's not all it's cracked up to be in the romance novels. Being cradled in some guy's arms close to his chest is one thing, although depending on what you have on, you do worry about what others might be able to see. When you're tossed over a shoulder, the shoulder starts to dig into your midsection and the blood rushing to your head can give you a headache."

Rook opened the side table next to the bed, grabbed the pen and notepad stored there, and jotted a few things down. "You never know what will give you some great details for a book."

"Sage does that too and it drives Roark nuts! Have you ever been behind the scenes here at the Savoy? Like going into some of the rooms?" Mazie said, finishing her breakfast and wiping her mouth with a napkin.

"No. Is that something you could arrange?"

"Yep. Give me a minute to get dressed and we can go do it now."

CHAPTER 14

Mazie dressed quickly and she and Rook opened the door to find an officer barring the way.

"I believe DSI Holmes wanted you to stay inside your rooms."

"That may be," said Rook, "but we're not under arrest and have done nothing wrong. So DSI Holmes can suggest, but he can't really make us do anything. My friend works here at the hotel and I'm a writer, so she was going to help me with some research."

"But DSI Holmes said…"

Rook crowded the officer's personal space. "I don't give a rat's ass what DSI Holmes said."

"And I'm ready to go. Officer, if it would make you feel better to accompany us, feel free to do so. I've got my security card here in my purse, let's go."

They breezed past the officer, who, not knowing what else to do, fell in behind them.

"Do you know much about the Savoy?" asked Mazie.

"Only that Sage Mathews has one of her fictional characters living here. Do people actually do that?"

"Yes, on both a short and long term basis. One of the things we're known for is our outstanding service. Taking care of our guests is our number one priority, and it's drilled into us from the first day we join the staff."

"I hear the hotel has good staff retention."

"We do, because upper management believes if they take care of us, we'll take better care of the guests. We are paid well, have excellent benefits, and there is a chance of advancement."

They stepped out into the lobby and Rook looked around like a child in wonder.

"I've heard about the Savoy and seen pictures, but this is my first time here. Last night they brought me up in the service elevator and I missed seeing all of this. It's amazing! The coffered ceilings, columns, the floors. It's just stunning."

Mazie laughed. "I work here and after a while, you don't really notice, but you're right, it's a gorgeous place to work or stay."

"I'd love that."

Mazie spent the next several hours walking Rook through the hotel, showing her both private and public spaces and letting her soak in the atmosphere. The novelist was scribbling notes in the pad at a furious pace.

"I can see why Sage used this place as a setting for some of her novels. It's gorgeous and so moody. Not in a bad way, but there's so much atmosphere here."

"Sage used to say the same thing. When a new Clive Thomas novel would come out, we'd all walk around reading it and looking at the various places both here in the hotel and at other various sites. We have people who come in and ask if we have a tour. The gal who used to be the full-time night concierge has reduced her regular schedule and has been asked if she'd like to develop and then conduct the tours. Nobody knows the hotel like Corinne."

"Sage has such a vivid imagination. I don't know that I could do something like her paranormal series. I swear to God, the way she describes things—a villa in Italy, a plantation outside of New Orleans, and that sex club here in London. It would be so cool if a place like that actually existed."

Mazie turned to the officer. "Could you give us a little space?" she asked, then waited for the officer to move away out of hearing distance. "You mean the BDSM club in the heart of London?"

"That's the one."

"It's based on a real one called Baker Street."

"Is it really?"

"There are several lifestyle clubs here in the city. Baker Street is the best."

"You sound like you have some experience in that."

"I do. I'm a member, and so is Holden. Actually, it's where we met."

"So, you're a—what do they call it? Submissive?"

Mazie nodded. "I am. Specifically, I'm Holden's submissive and he is my Dominant or Dom. We call submissives subs. The D is always capitalized as are the terms Sir or Master and the s is always lowercase."

"You don't exactly strike me as meek and mild," said Rook, raising her eyebrows at Mazie.

"I'm not, but then a common misconception is that subs are weak. But we're not. If checking it out interests you, I can ask JJ, the club owner, if I could take you on a tour when it isn't open. A lot of people don't want others to know they're members, so it would have to be when it was only staff."

"Isn't that where that K&R Security firm is headquartered?"

"Yes, 221A Baker Street is the home of Cerberus. I got told last night if I didn't settle down, instead of the Savoy, they could put me up at Baker Street, and I don't think they meant one of the luxury privacy suites. Rumor in the submissives' salon—that's kind of like our locker room—is that Cerberus has a couple of saferooms, as well as an interrogation room somewhere in the building."

"Wow," said Rook. "I had no idea that was all right here under my nose. I'd love to check it out sometime!"

"Sure," said Mazie. "I can set it up for you later."

They finished their tour and Mazie invited Rook back to the command center. She opened the door to her little sanctum. "This is where I spend most of my time."

"Whoa."

"The Savoy has some of the best security in the world. I can keep an eye on everything that's going on. If you want, we can have lunch in here."

"That would be great," said Rook.

They ordered lunch and again, delivery took longer than normal.

Mazie shook her head. "They've got to be driving the kitchen staff nuts."

"I've been thinking about something we talked about earlier. It really is kind of overkill to be this protective."

"I agree. I think the fact that someone tried to steal my bag and kept it in their possession for a few minutes spooked the Yard. It just felt too coincidental. They asked me about the kid in the hoodie who tried to steal it on the subway. They wondered if maybe he'd been here casing the place, but as you can see, I would have spotted him."

Lunch was delivered and Rook picked up her fork and tapped it on her plate. Mazie was beginning to realize how Rook kept her gorgeous figure. That morning, Rook's selections from the sampler had been things with no cheese, lots of veggies and a dry English muffin, avoiding butter, sauces and the delectable potatoes and breakfast meats. On the other hand, Mazie had enjoyed the eggs benedict and everything that had come with it. For lunch, Rook ordered the Caesar Salad with grilled chicken, and Mazie got the cheeseburger with bacon, gruyere, and sliced avocado. She didn't let it bother her, as Holden seemed to prefer her shape to tall, long, lean girls like Rook. But no, that wasn't it at all, she reminded herself. Holden loved her and got after her if she talked bad about herself.

"What are you thinking?" asked Rook.

"That watching you eat, I can see why you have such a gorgeous figure. Then I reminded myself that Holden loves me and likes me just the way I am."

Rook put her fork down. "I envy you that. Not just the Holden Tremayne part, but having someone who truly loves you for you. And you are not to interpret that as that there is anything wrong with the way you look."

"Thanks, I appreciate that."

"Do you think the gaming company knows that somebody is trying to rig the game? Do you think whoever's after us is also after any of the other teams?"

Dipping a French fry in ranch dressing, Mazie said, "I don't know that they'd target others, as we were the leaders. But you have to think that whoever is within striking position has to be a suspect, and if it isn't the second-place team, it's one of the other top-ranked teams."

"Do you know which team is in second place?" Suddenly Rook dropped her fork in surprise. "Oh my God! we haven't been checking for clues this whole time."

Mazie held up her wrist and checked her watch. "Not to worry. I have an alarm set on my watch. The second a clue drops, I'm on it."

"God, Holden was so right. You are the perfect person to be our coordinator."

"I did check the standings. I think the Yard has three groups of suspects. The second, third, and fourth place teams keep swapping places. We're the logical first target, as we're way out in front of everyone."

"Do we know who any of the members of the other alliances are?"

"I don't. And as far as I know, Holden only went looking for our profiles, not anyone else's. He knew each of us within the game and watched us play. I think he really wanted to make the proverbial dream team."

"And now Bishop is dead. I'm still having trouble wrapping my head around that."

There was a knock on the door, and a police officer walked in with Rook's laptop.

Rook reached out with both hands grasping, "Come to mama. Did they hurt you?"

The officer and Mazie both laughed at her. "What?" she said defensively. "This thing is my life. I back it up daily, more often if I had a long writing jag and got a lot done. Speaking of which, this has been great fun, but I'm kind of on a deadline."

"No problem. I'll let you know if a clue drops."

"You're the best, Fury," said Rook, heading toward the elevators.

The cop looked back and forth between them, "You can go with her," said Mazie. "I promise to stay locked in here and you can send someone back for me later."

"Thanks. Someone will be down right away." The officer closed the door and made a mad dash for the elevator bank.

∽

Sentience always returned moments before the granite began to crumble and fall away. The first couple of years it had been a challenge to not panic as he became aware of being entombed with no way to breathe. Over the centuries, he had learned to trust that he would be restored to his half-life each day as the sun set, only to have it snatched away as the sun began to rise the next morning. At first, he'd thought the witch's curse was to make him a monster, but he came to understand that he had always been a monster; the witch had merely allowed that to manifest itself. The real curse was to be immortal and to be alone forever.

After watching his beloved sister grow old and die as well as the rest of the Order of the Seven Maidens who'd fought to keep him safe, Holden had moved on, not forming any attachments as the pain of losing them was too great. Until Mazie. With Mazie he had been intrigued by her avatar, and not so much by her appearance, as there were millions of avatars of that archetype and few of them actually resembled the person who'd created them. No, it was the way her mind worked; the way she strategized, rarely making a wrong move and if she did, recovering quickly.

His senses were always acutely aware as he shed his sarcophagus at the end of the day. But tonight was different. Now he could feel the presence of another gargoyle—more than one, actually. As he became aware and was able to move, Holden remained the monster he'd become and rolled away from the threat, sweeping his strong, reptilian-like tail at the feet of whatever threat was there. He rolled up onto his feet and into a defensive stance and eyed the three gargoyles who had thought to kill him all those years ago. The purebloods. He had to give it to them that they had their own kind of honor—they hadn't tried to kill him while he slept.

"We told you to be gone," said their tall, muscular leader with a protruding brow and small horns sprouting from his forehead. "You were a fool to return."

"I hate to break it to you," said Holden, "but I never left."

Holden had learned there were three main differences between purebloods and cursedborn. As long as purebloods avoided sunlight, they could avoid being turned to stone, and purebloods could not shapeshift —their form remained the same. And finally, purebloods tended to be fairly simple and stupid. Holden remained in his grotesque form. As strong as he was as a human, he was even more powerful as a gargoyle.

"Now, you die!" shouted one of the other gargoyles, lifting a warclub over his head and charging. The other companion gargoyle rushed to follow him, a Roman short sword in his hand.

Holden looked around for something with which to defend himself. He spotted a length of sturdy pipe and crouched low, sweeping his tail a second time, knocking their feet out from beneath them and rendering them stunned. Their leader roared again and swung a broadsword around and over his head like some kind of stiff, double-edged, demented lariat. Holden threw himself toward the pipe and managed to grasp it and roll just out of reach as the lead Gargoyle raised the weapon to attack again.

"Be gone!" thundered a strong, female voice, accompanied by the crackle of a lightning bolt. "Your kind have never been welcomed at the Savoy—be it palace, hospital or hotel."

The three gargoyles hissed and brandished their weapons but did not advance on the beautiful Irish woman who had to be a witch. Holden released his hold on his gargoyle form. He had no doubt the witch had counted four monsters on the roof so to try and convince her he was wholly human would be a mistake. But he shifted and left only his wings to mark him as something other than human. After all, it would be easier to fly away if his wings were immediately available, although he'd once shifted mid-air and used them to glide to a soft landing on the ground.

"Quit your bitching and leave this place before I turn you all into one-eyed toads."

The gargoyles growled and snarled but backed away. Despite their bluster and threats, the purebloods retreated to the edge of the roof, flapped their great wings, and flew away, lifting themselves high overhead so as not to be spotted from the ground below.

The witch turned and looked at him. "Cursed-born," she said matter-of-factly.

"Aye. I'm Holden Tremayne."

She laughed. "I guess that's why you're so camera shy and never seen during the day. What are you doing here, Tremayne? You and your kind don't normally trouble us here at the Savoy."

"Those," he said, disdainfully pointing at the departing gargoyles, "are not my kind nor would they think kindly of you for labeling them so."

"I'm Saoirse Spenser. Do you fold your wings under? Or…" She peered at his shoulders.

"No, I can retract them along with my other gargoyle characteristics." As he spoke, he did so and crossed to where he'd been perched all day. He grabbed his things, donned his shirt, and shoved the rest in his pockets. "Unlike those who wanted to kill me, I can shapeshift when I am awake."

"And the purebloods can't? I'll bet that pisses them off."

Holden chuckled, beginning to relax and feel as though the witch meant him no harm. "If they can stay out of the sunlight, they don't turn to stone. Given that cursedborn are completely vulnerable in that state, it's something of a tradeoff."

"So, what are you doing up here on the Savoy's roof? It isn't at all normal for one of your kind to be up here."

"I tarried too long in the moonlight and knew I didn't have time to return to my normal perch. I meant no insult or disrespect, just needed to find a safe place to hide."

"That explains the roof, but what are you doing at the Savoy?"

She was smart and not easily baited by another line of questioning.

"I was here with a friend last evening. One who is in danger. I wanted to protect her."

Before he could think of how to convince her he was no threat to her or the others at the hotel without implicating Mazie, she cut him off. "The two women the Yard has stashed here?"

Holden nodded. "So, you know enough to know my presence and your discretion are needed."

"I have no wish to quarrel with you. My husband is the head of guest services here at the hotel."

Recognition dawned. "Of course, Felix and Saoirse Spenser. You play at Baker Street."

"Holy shit. Gabe said you were a member as well, and so is another staff..." The witch shook her head. "Please don't tell me you were with Mazie Bridges."

"She is my woman and my sub."

"And has no bloody idea that you're a gargoyle."

Holden resented her assumption and shifted his weight from one foot to the other. "You don't know that."

Saoirse laughed. "Oh, but I do. If Mazie knew you were a gargoyle and vulnerable during the day, she'd have been sitting up here at your feet"

"Like a proper sub?"

The witch laughed again. "No, Tremayne. She'd have been here with a shotgun, protecting your stony ass. Oh God, what a clusterfuck. Although it does explain why she got so dodgy with Spense earlier. You may as well come along. We'll need to get this sorted with Holmes."

"I fear telling him my secret will only confuse and frighten him."

"Hardly. I don't know that a gargoyle is going to faze him at all. Trust me, you wouldn't be the strangest or nastiest thing that goes bump in the night that he's encountered, not even in the last couple of months. Let's go, cursedborn," said the witch as she headed back to the access door, her laughter trailing behind her.

CHAPTER 15

Mazie had happily worked part of the afternoon in the command center. The security team had been short-staffed ever since Gabe had left. She had to admit that while she wished them well, she would have liked it if they hadn't emigrated to America. She'd enjoyed working for him and having Anne mentor her as a sub would have been incredible. Anne was the kind of sub she wanted to be. Nobody messed with Anne other than Gabe, and he had an indulgent streak for his wife that was a mile wide.

The officers hadn't been happy about her working, but as she'd pointed out, the command center was every bit as safe as one of the rooms—maybe even safer. But they'd insisted on posting guards—one outside and one inside with her. She'd thought about being a hard ass about the fact that no one but authorized hotel personnel could be in the heart of the Savoy's electronic security but had decided that Holden would most likely not consider that as being cooperative. She was hoping that he wouldn't be too annoyed that she'd taken Rook on a tour of the hotel, and that they'd had lunch in here.

Glancing at her watch, she told the officer, "I'm about ready to wrap it up for the day. I want to get upstairs and take a shower and change before Holden gets back."

She was just about to leave when an email came in addressed to her Savoy email address. No big deal, it wasn't a secret that she worked here. All emails were processed through the hotel's anti-virus and malware system and if they weren't completely clean, they got passed into a special inbox to be more closely examined. Mazie double-clicked on the email, then jumped to her feet and stepped back as if she'd released a live venomous snake into the room.

"Miss Bridges? Are you all right?" asked the officer. "Should I get someone?"

Mazie nodded, taking a deep breath. "Please tell the Yard they're going to want to get someone from your Cyber Crime Unit down here. And could you ask the head concierge to contact Eddy Chastain? He's the partner of one of our other staff members. Eddy is an expert in electronics and security."

"Sure, but what should I tell them?"

Mazie turned and looked at her. "That I have

received a credible death threat. I think you should alert your people upstairs to get eyes on Rook. If you like, I can dispatch my people as well."

"No, we'll take care of Ms. Butler."

"Good enough." Mazie tapped her com button. "Savoy Security, Code 3. I repeat, Code 3."

"What the hell is Code 3 and why are you getting your people involved?"

"You may well be responsible for Rook's security and welfare, but I'm responsible for the staff and guests of this hotel. Code 3 is the call sign for an electronic threat to the hotel. My people will divide into two teams—one will have the entrances and exits covered within minutes and will ensure that we know everyone who tries to come in or leave this hotel. The other will make a sweep of the building with scanners."

The officer left, leaving the other one standing outside the door. "I hate to be rude, but I need you to come in or out. I need to lock that door." The officer stepped inside. "Thank you."

"You're awfully calm, considering."

"I trained to join the Yard, and my training after I joined the Savoy has been extensive. Gabriel Watson wanted every single one of us to know just what to do and how to react in any given situation."

"But I thought the threat was to you personally," said the officer.

"It was, but it doesn't matter. We handle the threat

to someone's life in the exact same way no matter who's in danger, whether it's a bellhop or Her Majesty."

Mazie sat down in her chair. Well, so much for dinner with Holden. He was going to freak. She knew she'd need to soothe the savage beast and the best way to do that was with sex. She wondered if the officer would mind stepping outside while she either went down on Holden or offered up her pussy for his use? She'd let him know she would service him in the best way possible to ease his concern.

She looked down at the email. Short, succinct, and to the point. There was a picture of the tarot card with the picture of her avatar and threatening words below it:

> I tried to warn you.
> Bishop died in vain.
> I should have killed you first.
> Lesson learned; corrective action
> will be taken

Her avatar had been garroted. "Okay, asshole. I'm not as good as Eddy or Holden, but I can try to get you locked out of our system."

How the hell had the damn thing gotten through? The first thing she wanted Eddy to do was to check the Savoy's computer systems, starting with the guest registry, personnel files and financials. Everything else after that.

Mazie began checking the systems one by one. She was glad that before he'd left, Gabe had hired Eddy to do a complete overhaul of the hotel's system. No expense had been spared. Banks in Geneva were more vulnerable than the Savoy. Mazie grinned when she thought of Corinne's boyfriend—Eddy was going to be pissed.

There was a knock on the door and after verifying the identity of the person on the other side, the officer allowed three more officers to enter the room.

"DSI Holmes is on his way, and he wants you upstairs in your room."

"That may well be what he wants, but as my friend pointed out earlier today, I am not under arrest and not subject to your authority. I understand what your job and your priorities are, but they are not mine. I need to be here to coordinate things until our cyber consultant gets here and my boss, who is the head of guest services, tells me they have things in hand. You can have two people in here if you like, but I need to check in with my people."

Mazie turned her back, ignoring the police officers to focus on the job at hand. She went through and checked with each of her team members—they were doing their jobs and doing them well.

"Mazie," said Felix Spenser as he entered the

command center with the hotel's general manager in tow. "Bring us up to speed."

"Last night a member of an online alliance I'm a part of was murdered. The Yard brought two of us here for safekeeping, as it didn't appear the killer knew who the fourth member of our team was. The murderer used pictures of our avatars but addressed Rook's and mine to us personally. We've been here under guard all day. I came down to try to keep from falling so far behind with work.

"There was an email addressed to me that had made it through our filters, so I opened it. That's all I've done, and I've been watching the system since then. Personnel and Finance have been told to shut down and not to use the system. I alerted Scotland Yard and asked that you let Eddy know he was needed. I can't imagine any virus, worm, or other malware getting through his firewalls, traps, and security measures."

"Well done, Mazie. Gabe would be proud. I've called Eddy. He and Corinne were on their way over to meet Saoirse and I for dinner, so he should be here any time."

"Excellent job, Ms. Bridges," said the GM. "I think these officers should get you back up to your room. We'll be posting for a replacement for Gabriel. I do hope you'll be applying."

Mazie looked at him. "Thank you, sir. I will." She turned to Spense. "Don't let anyone touch anything."

Spense smiled. "Gabe trained you well. Maybe you and Ms. Butler might think about joining us for dinner."

"I'd like nothing more, but being in any of the restaurants would be problematic and might erode the experience for our other guests. I'd suggest one of the rooms, but they'd be too small. We could make one of the private meeting rooms work though. The Sorcerer Room might work. It would be out of the way and the kitchen would have an easier time working with the Yard about the food. Maybe have them prepare a family-style menu."

"You think quick on your feet," said the GM. "Felix, take care of it. Ms. Bridges, why don't you head up to your room and when the Sorcerer Room is secure, we'll have the officers bring you and Ms. Butler down."

"I have a friend staying with me, sir. DSI Holmes knows him and has approved his being here."

"Well, if Holmes has approved, that's good enough for me." The GM headed out the door. Just as he was about to exit, he stopped and turned back. "Don't think I haven't noticed that while the police wanted you safe, you insisted on being down here to ensure the safety of the hotel and direct the security team. As I said, well done."

Mazie happily accompanied the officers upstairs. After they cleared her room, she went in, stripped down and stepped under the shower. When she came out, she dried her hair, applied makeup, and stepped into one of her outfits. Whoever had packed for her had obviously noted Holden was with her and had packed accordingly. She owed the woman a gift certificate from the hotel. The woman had packed some of the things she'd picked up the first day she'd met Rook and after she'd begun training and playing at Baker Street.

She put on an off-the-shoulder black knit dress. It hugged her curves but wasn't tight. It was relatively short, but not obscenely so. Mazie added a wide leather belt buckled at an angle, and red kitten heels, because everyone knew nothing bad ever happened when you were wearing red shoes. She added funky earrings and a bangle bracelet and took a good long look in the full-length mirror. The short dress made the most of her height, the fabric clung but moved with her easily. The earrings set off her graceful neck and her great haircut. All in all, she had to admit she looked damn fine.

Now to wait for Holden.

―

Holden followed the Irish witch down the stairs. "How did you know they were up there?"

"Spense was working late so I came by to have dinner with him. I felt something funny in the energy, something that didn't belong. I went downstairs to check the basement, as the last time we had something off in the energy, it was down there. When there wasn't anything there and the disruption felt less intense, I figured it was probably the roof."

"And your husband just gave you his permission to come up here and deal with whatever supernatural forces were waiting? Not my idea of a Dom."

Saoirse whirled and sent a blast of pure energy at him, causing him to stagger. She seemed surprised that it hadn't knocked him off his feet. Gargoyles—even cursedborn—were heavier in mass than humans of a comparable size.

"For your information, I didn't ask him, and next time you speak ill of my husband, it won't be pure white energy I send, but lightning."

Holden found himself growing to like the witch. "My apologies. I am worried about Mazie."

"Mazie is in the Savoy and can take care of herself. She's surrounded by men who would never let anything hurt her in any way, shape, or form."

He realized they were no longer talking about whoever it was that had killed Bishop.

"Duly noted."

"So, how'd you get this way and when?" she asked, weaving her way through the equipment that was stored just below the roof.

"Thirteenth century, and by one of *your* kind." When she whirled around, he raised his hand. "Again, my apologies. I long ago reconciled what the witch had done to me. She thought I had wronged her sister, who then committed suicide. I never believed the unborn child was mine, but I'd like to think that even back then, had I known she would kill herself I would have done the right thing."

"And now?"

"I make sure that the possibility of conceiving a child is negligible before I play."

"Good man. And is that all you're doing with Mazie?"

Holden chuckled. "Nay, Saoirse. Mazie is my woman and my sub for as long as she will have me, or until we are parted by death."

Saoirse stopped and looked at him. "Then before you go further, she needs to know about you being cursedborn."

Holden stopped and shook his head. "No." He considered lying to Saoirse, but he was done with lying. It had never served him well and it would do no good now. "I didn't expect to get involved with her. I assembled a team to play an online game in real life, then we met and connected at Baker Street."

"So? What stupid man thing did you do? I swear, the lot of you have testosterone poisoning."

He chuckled. "Actually, that might be a better explanation. But I didn't know what to do, so I told the alliance that I'd been hurt. I was trying to buy myself a few weeks for her to get to know me."

"So, in other words, you damn well knew who she was and didn't tell her."

Holden blew out a breath. "Basically, yes."

"Idiot," she said scornfully before blasting him with another energy ball.

It felt like she'd punched him in the gut, but he took it as a good sign that it had merely been white energy and not lightning. He fell in behind her until they got to the service elevator, where he pushed the call button for her.

"Who was she?"

"The girl or the witch? Actually, it doesn't matter. I don't think I ever knew and it's long past the time I could have remembered."

"Where did you get cursed?" asked Saoirse.

"At Castle Tremayne in Cornwall. It's a ruin now."

"They let you live?"

"No. My father tried to kill me, he wanted to destroy me in my stone form."

"Then how did you survive?"

Holden smiled. "My sister, Morwenna."

"Morwenna of the Order of the Seven Maidens?" asked Saoirse incredulously.

"Do you know of my sister?"

"I do. Recently, my friends and I came to know of the Order—both their history and how they exist and operate in the modern world—I've been doing some research about them. Your sister figured prominently in my research. She looked for a cure, you know. For your curse. She tried to find the witch who did it and when that failed, she tried to find a way to reverse it."

"Can you do that? Reverse it?"

"I don't know. Can you remember the exact words she used?"

Holden nodded. "One doesn't tend to forget the words that damned one to immortality."

"Write them down for me. I'll do a little research and see what I can find. You know, there are those who say immortality would be a blessing."

"They are wrong. To watch those you love grow old and die is no blessing. I've come to believe that the sweetest thing in this world would be to grow old alongside the woman I love and to die holding each other as we pass from this life to the next."

"I take it that's what you would like to do with Mazie."

"I would ask no more of this life than that."

CHAPTER 16

*A*s they stepped off the service elevator they were greeted by uniformed officers.

"Shit," said Saoirse. "Whatever it is, I guarantee you Spense has texted me. I'm going to catch hell for not keeping my electronic leash turned on."

"What's wrong?" asked Holden just as Holmes stepped off a regular passenger elevator.

"I just got here," said Holmes, speaking into a com unit. "Spense, I have Saoirse." There was a pause. "I'll make sure to deliver her into your loving arms." He tapped the com unit. "You had your phone turned off again. I wouldn't fancy your chances for sitting too comfortably tonight."

"Seriously, Holmes?" Saoirse said, looking around.

"No one but the three of us can hear me and Holden's a Dom at Baker Street."

"Holmes, what happened?" growled Holden.

"Everything is under control. But Mazie received a death threat from the killer."

"What the fuck is wrong with you people? I thought you were supposed to be guarding her," Holden snapped as he ran down the hall.

"Let him through!" called Holmes from behind him.

The hall wasn't overly long, and Holden sprinted it easily, being shown into her room as soon as he got there. He caught her up in his arms and held her close.

"Are you all right?"

"I'm fine, Holden. When I first opened the email it spooked me, but then I realized it was just an email. I had them call Holmes and I dispatched our security team. The GM was impressed."

Holden glanced around the room. There was no desktop, no laptop. "You did that from your phone?"

"No, I was downstairs in the command center."

"You were what?" he growled, turning her loose. He stalked back to the door and jerked it open just as Holmes started to enter. "What the fuck was she doing down in the command center?"

"According to her detail, neither she nor Ms. Butler were inclined to be compliant with our request to stay in their rooms or even together in one room. I just talked to Spense, they're setting up dinner for you two, Ms. Butler, Spense, Saoirse, Eddy and Corinne, and someone called my wife, so Rachel and I were downstairs. The officers have cleared the room and we are to head down."

"What kind of time do I have?" Holden asked Holmes, trying to get a rein on his anger, which was being fueled by fear.

"Not that kind of time. Don't worry about it. As I always tell Rachel, discipline can wait until the proper time and place. Your girl's dressed up and everybody's waiting. Let's go have some dinner, talk about what we know including the email our killer sent Mazie, and where we go from here. Then you can bring her back up here and slap her ass silly."

Holden turned back to her and held out his hand. "You heard the man. We need to be downstairs. Make no mistake, we will discuss this later."

"Maybe I would prefer my own company," Mazie said, drawing herself up. Holden growled—an honest to goodness growl. Deciding discretion was the better part of valor, she continued, "But then again maybe not."

Holden tried to hold onto his anger but couldn't. Mazie was fearless, maybe even a touch reckless, but she definitely wasn't stupid. She took his hand and matched his stride as they headed for the elevator. "I like the dress," he said. "You look beautiful."

She gave him a demure smile. "Thank you."

They met Rook at the elevator and went down as

a group, surrounded by uniformed police officers. They made their way to the Sorcerer room, the smallest and most intimate of the hotel's private dining and meeting spaces. Created in the 1920s from two storage closets, it could only seat about ten people comfortably. With its distinctive dark red walls and unique furnishings, the room was cozy and felt more like the dining room or study in a private home as opposed to a meeting space in a large, luxurious hotel.

Police officers were escorting waitstaff holding large platters of food. "I suggested family-style," offered Mazie.

"Thank you," said Holmes. "That made it easier on the security detail."

They entered the room, and each took a seat at the large round table, making themselves comfortable as the waitstaff set up the room. Holden chuckled as Holmes literally delivered the Irish witch into her husband's hands. No doubt about it, the witch had been warned more than once by her husband about turning her mobile off. He'd need to let Mazie know he expected her to keep her mobile with her and turned on as well.

∽

"Fair warning," said Mazie. She pointed to Rook. "My friend Samantha Butler, also known as Rook, is a writer and given to taking copious notes. And the gentleman to my right is Holden Tremayne..."

"And I am her lover and her Dom," he interjected as if daring her to contradict him.

If he wanted to play it brazenly, she had no problem with that. "My lover, Dom, and Master. Holden, Rook, and I were part of an alliance with the man who was murdered. We knew him by his online name of Bishop. As far as I'm concerned, we're still involved in a real-life quest with a half a million dollars as the prize." Mazie turned to Holmes. "You're probably more up-to-speed than I am. Why don't you take over?"

Holmes nodded. "Bishop, whose real name was Elvis Sanders, was either forcibly pushed or thrown from the roof of a building last night. As far as we can tell, he was lured up there by his killer. We believe the killer to be one of four other groups in the game that rounded up the top five. Speaking with the game owners, only this top five really have a chance at winning, unless all five groups were either eliminated or dropped out. We do believe intimidation is a big goal for the killer as it should narrow his field fairly quickly.

"We've been able to start narrowing down our suspects in this pool of people. We have detectives searching for other possible motives, but it seems most likely Bishop was killed to try and get the Phantom

Guild here to quit. I have to tell you that with the receipt of the death threat against Mazie, we will be focusing almost exclusively on the suspects who are playing the game"

"How did you do that?" asked Rook, her pen at the ready.

Holmes shook his head. "Some alibied out and some we could eliminate based on the forensics associated with how Bishop was killed. Regardless of whether he was pushed or thrown, the person who did it had to have a certain amount of upper body strength as well as be a certain height. For instance, Tailspin is a petite elderly lady who has arthritis. By the way, Knight Fury—that's Mazie—she's a huge fan of yours and hopes you, and I quote, 'kick some arse.' There is no way, unless she hired someone to do it, that she's our killer. We also checked her bank records and there was nothing to indicate she paid to have someone else do the deed.

"We've been able to reach most of the members of three teams, but the Baskerville Brigade seems unwilling to talk to us and has been pretty elusive. We did reach one guy by the name of Jack Peterboro, who was helpful but not. He said the group has never met and he can only contact them through the game."

"That can't be right," said Mazie.

"How so?" asked Holden.

"The top five alliances were all there for the first challenge—the key challenge. The Phantom Guild has been in the lead from the start. The next four teams have all remained in the Top Five but have changed around in their placings. It seems to me the killer has to be in one of those teams or the team in its entirety. We're checking now with the game owners to get the real names of those four other teams."

"Where are you going with this?" asked Holmes.

"They had to be there that morning when Hyde Park opened. And all of the alliances had at least two members of their alliance present. The game is moving fast. The first clue dropped and there was a deadline of ninety-six hours. Anyone who hadn't claimed a key by then was removed from the game. The second clue was about seventy-two hours later, and the rest will be every thirty-six to forty hours after that."

Rook nodded. "We were down a man—Holden told us he was injured." She pointed at Holden and said, "I think you should know you can go to hell for lying as well as stealing, just saying. Anyway, Bishop, Fury, and I have been alternating who is actually going after the clues, according to our schedules. We figure out the clue as a group, usually with Knight there calling in. Then we go after the clue in the physical world as a pair, never alone."

"That was a rule we agreed upon after Holden and I got together. I'm still surprised I didn't figure this out beforehand. You were playing us from the very first."

"We had this disagreement last night. We both agreed I was wrong. But the fact is, from the first night we were together, I have acted like your Dom and so I made sure you were safe. Get over it. My default will always be to keep you safe, regardless of whether you like it or not."

"You know," said Eddy, "depending on how good this guy from the Baskerville Brigade is, some of the members might not exist at all. He could have fake accounts set up and be playing them from a massive computer setup—not unlike the one here at the Savoy. If he has the skill, he could set up and play as each of the Avatars. Or it could be the one guy you can find and another one or two who are doing the same."

"One of our guys liked the Archie Alliance. He said they seem especially aggressive, attacking everybody."

"They would be my least likely suspect. They're grievers—players who attack for sport, as opposed to points or an advantage in the game," explained Eddy.

"I agree," said Mazie. "They've been around for a long time and mainly seem to get their kicks from giving people a bad time."

"But didn't you have a bad run-in with them?" asked Rook.

Mazie nodded. "A couple of months ago. I ended up skunking the whole lot of them though. I stole their mojo bags. They were pissed. So, I could see them coming after me, but why kill Bishop?"

"I think we can all agree," said Holden, "that Bishop was a warning. Would someone mind telling me what was said in the threatening email Mazie received? And how did it get to her?"

"That's not important," said Mazie, trying to dismiss the issue.

"It is to me," said Holden.

"He sent her an email which read," said Eddy, ignoring the fact that Mazie was glaring at him with a death-ray stare, "I tried to warn you. Bishop died in vain. I should have killed you first. Lesson learned; corrective action will be taken."

"I agree that sounds frightening," said Rook.

"It was emailed directly to me here at the hotel. Not only did the threat get past the security system that scans every email for keywords, but it also means he knows my name, where I work, and that I was working today."

"Oh shit," said Rook.

"Precisely," said Holden.

"Holden, I'll find this guy," vowed Eddy. "I'm putting everything else on hold."

"Thanks, Eddy."

"In fact," Eddy said, "I'd better get back to it. Are you working tonight, sweetheart?"

Corinne smiled. "I'm pretty sure that was

addressed to me. I am. We're a bit short-handed right now so I've been covering some of the extra shifts."

"Which I appreciate," said Spense.

"I need to get Rachel home and do some paperwork from the house," said Holmes, standing up and pulling Rachel's chair back. "Miss Butler, can I escort you back to your room?"

"Thank you. I am a bit tired," she answered.

When those in the room had been narrowed down to four, Mazie looked across the table at Spense. "Well, that was about as subtle as a freight train."

"There are things you need to know about your Dom," said Saoirse, "*before* you accept his collar or go to bed with him again, for that matter."

Holden growled. "I was planning to tell her."

"Then you and I have no problem. Regardless of what happens, I will talk to the Order and see if I can't help you."

Mazie looked across at Spense. "Why is it I get the feeling that of the four of us, I'm the only one who doesn't know what you're talking about?"

"I believe, Tremayne, that's your cue," said Spense pointedly.

Mazie looked between the two men. "What is it?" Holden was tight-lipped and silent, just like his avatar. "Who is the Order and what is it Saoirse is going to do for you?"

"You tell her, or I will," said Spense.

"This is not the way I wanted to tell her," growled Holden.

"And how and when did you plan to tell her?" said Spense with a growly tone all his own. "When you had a collar around her neck and were balls-deep in her?

CHAPTER 17

That was precisely when and how Holden had planned to tell her, but there was no way he was admitting to that, if for no other reason than Mazie was likely to go batshit crazy on him. He'd wanted to tell her when he was buried so deep in her that she couldn't get away.

"Quit growling at him and talk to me," implored Mazie. "Holden, what is it?"

They'd left him no way out. He'd meant to tell her the truth, but her friends seemed to think it was now or never, and Holden suspected they'd engineered it that way. He had to stop thinking about all that could go wrong. Forget that he'd lied to her… again. But then again, other than he'd known who she was before she'd known who he was, and the fact that he was a gargoyle, he'd never once lied to her, and he'd already come clean about one of those things before they'd slept together.

Granted the whole being a gargoyle that was born in the Thirteenth century thing was probably fairly substantial as withheld information went. But he hadn't technically lied to her. After all, she'd never asked him his birthdate or if he could shapeshift. He'd been very up-front and honest with her about what he wanted from her and about his feelings for her. Surely that counted for something.

He could still make things right. He could be completely straight with her and swear he'd never lie to her again. Oh wait, he'd done that last night, although as he'd already been withholding that information, was it really another lie. Or was it just the perpetuation of the old one?

"Holden? What are you going to tell me, that you're a vampire? It would explain why you can only see me at night," joked Mazie.

There was dead silence. No way to ease into this. No way to make it easier on both of them. Time to just rip the bandage off.

"Not a vampire. They are truly vile creatures with no sense of honor. They feed off people's life force and turn people without their consent," said Holden.

"True that," said Saoirse.

"Okay, this is really not funny. There's no such thing as vampires or werewolves or other nasty things that go bump in the night. Next thing you're going to tell me is that you're an alien come to conquer earth using a video game."

Taking a deep breath, Holden said, "I'm one of those other nasty things that go bump in the night. As you know, my name is Holden Tremayne. My father was the Duke of Cornwall, and I was born in the Thirteenth Century."

"Sure you were. I have to say, you look great for your age," teased Mazie, looking between the three of them. "Seriously not amusing."

"I'm being serious, Mazie. Back then I was a rounder or a bit of a lad—I spent my days riding, drinking, hunting, and whoring. Whatever suited me and with whomever I fancied. I lived only to please myself."

"Okay, now I know you're giving me a load of shit. That doesn't sound like you at all!"

"Watch your language."

"Are you kidding me? You're giving me some line of bullshit and you want to tell me to watch my language?"

"He's not joking, Mazie," said Saoirse gently. "You know about me—that I'm a witch."

"Yeah, so? You make salves and natural medicines and help people. I mean, it's not like you cast spells and send people to hell."

"Actually, I've done that a couple of times in the last year. Regardless of whether you believe me, you must believe Holden. He is who he says he is." She turned to Holden. "Tell her the rest, or I won't help you."

"You said you would regardless of what happened," challenged Holden.

"I lied. Tell her."

Mazie took both his hands in hers. "Tell me, please."

"As I said, I didn't always lead a life I could be proud of. One day there was a girl in a tavern who was a pretty little thing and gave every indication that not only did she want me to bed her, she had experience. I knew the moment my cock tore her maidenhead to shreds she'd lied about the second part. I still believe the first. I may have been the first, but I sure as hell wasn't the last. Her tips increased exponentially. I'm not saying she was a whore, but she liked sex and didn't mind a fellow giving her a little extra on the bill to enjoy himself between her legs."

Mazie pulled her hands away. Holden let her. "About seven months later, she showed up at my father's castle, heavy with child. She insisted I marry her. I wasn't interested in marrying anyone, especially a woman carrying the bastard of another man. I only had her the one time, and I know it could have happened then, but if it had been me, she would have been closer to term. I don't think she bedded me for my money, but I think when she was faced with having a child out of wedlock, she decided I was her best prospect."

"What did you do?" Mazie whispered.

"Not what you're thinking," said Holden wearily. "I didn't do anything but send her away, telling her I didn't believe her. It was not my finest hour. I knew for a fact that I wasn't the only one she'd been intimate with."

He closed his eyes. "All these centuries later, I can still see her on the edge of the cliff, right before it happened. I can hear her shouting to me, imploring me to marry her. I swear to God, if I'd known she would kill herself and the babe, I would have stepped up. At least I hope I would have, but I didn't know. It never crossed my mind that she'd take one more step back and allow herself to fall to the rocks and the sea below."

"How could you?" Mazie whispered.

"I was young and arrogant. I didn't believe the child was mine and I sure as hell never believed she'd kill herself. The next night her sister built a bonfire in the spot she'd tumbled from and cursed me. By day, I sleep in a sarcophagus of stone. Not like a vampire in a coffin, but totally encased in granite, not seeing, not hearing, not knowing what's going on all around me."

"Where do you hide this marble casket of yours?" Mazie asked sarcastically.

"Not a casket, not even a true sarcophagus. As the moon sets and the sun starts to rise, I begin to shift from living creature to monster and then from monster to stone."

"You're not a monster, Holden. She needs to understand that. Not all of your kind are evil."

"What the fuck are you talking about?" said Mazie, desperate for understanding.

"I transform from a man into a gargoyle, or grotesque. I become a stone gargoyle. Normally, I hide amongst the other true gargoyles at Westminster Abbey, but last night I stayed too long and knew I couldn't make it back, so I found a place here, up on the roof. Saoirse found me there."

"Three other gargoyles were trying to kill him," said Saoirse soothingly. "Just because you're not pureblood?"

Holden nodded. "Purebloods, those who are born gargoyles and have no other shape, hate those like me. They call us cursedborn, because we were once man and now we are gargoyle."

"You are still man by night."

"Yes. And when we are awake, we can shift between the two forms. I've learned to control certain aspects of my body. I've done it for so long, that usually the spikes or ridges along my spine, the two horns on my head, and my tail all retreat. I've trained myself to let the wings stay, in case I need to escape."

"Let me get this straight," said Mazie. "During the day you hang out at Westminster as a stone gargoyle and at night you come alive and hang out at Baker Street wielding a flogger and fucking? Seriously? Come on, Holden, you can't really expect me to believe all this."

"Spense, if you could guard the door and Saoirse, if you could pull the drapes?" asked Holden.

They did so and he removed his shirt, calling forth his great wings. All the color drained from Mazie's face.

"It's still me, Mazie. I just have wings. I'd love to soar over the city with you cradled in my arms. I'd love to sweep you down below the sea cliffs and flirt with the waves."

"No," she said, shaking her head.

"Yes," he said, kneeling in front of her and taking her hands into his own. "I am real." Holding on to her hands tightly, he shifted into a gargoyle, complete with misshapen head and spine. He held the form for a moment and then let it all recede until only the man was left behind.

Mazie stood up and backed away from him. "I don't know what bullshit kind of practical joke this is, but I don't like it. I'm out. I'll post in the game chat that I'm withdrawing from the game. That'll take the target off my back. Don't you ever come near me again. That goes for all of you. I quit. I don't want to be part of some freakshow."

She shoved Spense out of her way and Holden ran after her. "Leave her be," called Saoirse before he got to the door.

Holden looked at Spense. "My woman. My sub." He glanced over his shoulder at Saoirse.

Spense nodded. "But if you hurt her…"

"On my honor," answered Holden as he raced after her and the two officers chasing behind her.

~

Mazie flew out of the room. She had to be seeing things, or it was an optical illusion, or some kind of magick. Whatever it was, she wanted no part of it. When he'd first started telling her, she thought it had to be some kind of sick, twisted joke or a way to break up with her. After all, guys who looked like Holden Tremayne and had his kind of money didn't fall for short, curvy girls, they fell for women who looked like Rook. She was brokenhearted. All her dreams had come falling down with the sound of shattering glass.

She got to the service entrance of the hotel and turned on the cops. "Back off. You have no legal reason to hold me. "I'm done. Leave me alone."

Mazie pushed past them and left the building, wishing to God she hadn't had on these stupid heels. And where the fuck was she going without her purse? She had to go back and get her things. Without her purse she had no way home, no way back to her *pied-á-terre*, back to her safe little life.

Her sudden about-face caused her to slam straight into Holden's chest.

"Mazie, it isn't safe for you out there. If you can't deal with what I am, I understand. But there's no reason for you to endanger yourself or leave your job or Baker Street."

"Don't! God, why do you have to be so fucking understanding. How could you do this to me… again! You let me believe last night that everything was okay, but today it's hey by the way, I'm a gargoyle. I just… I just can't."

Holden wrapped her in his arms, pulling her close and trapping her against his muscular chest. Mazie pushed against him. The winner of the fight was a foregone conclusion. He crushed her to him, her breasts hard against him. He grabbed her face and gently placed his hand under her chin to tilt her head back so that his mouth could descend on hers in a savage kiss.

She wanted to fight, wanted to deny him—do anything that would allow her pride to believe that he simply overpowered her, but she knew it wasn't true. She wanted this, wanted him. She couldn't believe the intense level of need she felt for this man, not just physically, but deep in her soul. His tongue plunged into her mouth, plundering it and setting a match to her arousal that burst into a flame and then into a wildfire.

"We need to talk," said Holden once they'd come up for air.

"We have nothing to say to each other. Like I said,

I'm out. I don't know what sick games you and your friends are up to, but I'm out of those too. I refuse to have anything more to do with you."

"I can't allow that. You are my responsibility."

"Says who?"

"I do, until I know you are safe."

Holden hustled her into the service elevator and hit the button for the top floor. She was caged in his arms and there was little she could do about it. Worse yet, if she was being honest, she didn't want to do anything about it. Once they were at the top floor storage space, Holden dragged her behind him until they were out on the roof. In the three years she had worked at the Savoy, she'd never been on the roof. Truth was, she wasn't overly fond of hcights.

"This is my world, Mazie. The moon and the night sky. For close to seven hundred years, I have existed in this world, but I haven't lived in it."

There was a sound like a leather coat being thrown open. She looked up to see his great wings reaching past the top of his head. She gasped.

"They are a part of me, as is the stone creature that sleeps by day and wanders by night. I had long ago accepted that it was part and parcel of the curse. There have been so many times that I wished that somehow, I had been a better man—less arrogant, less concerned with my own needs and more concerned with the needs of others. Less like my father and more like my sister. You would have liked Morwenna, and she would have adored you."

She couldn't help herself. "What happened to her?"

"She defied my father and refused to marry as he wanted her to." His eyes warmed the way they did when he stroked her cheek and kissed her tenderly. "She drugged the guards he had set on her door and escaped our castle. She ran for the one place she knew would give her shelter—the Order of the Seven Maidens."

"A cloister?"

"Once it was, yes. But Viking raiders destroyed all that with their raping and pillaging. The church, the surrounding town folk, and the Knights Templar all decreed the women unclean. They all believed the sisters should have committed some kind of ritual suicide. But the nuns chose their own faith, rebuilt, and declared themselves free of men. And they were, until I turned to stone and my father thought to end me."

"Oh my God, Holden, that's awful."

She shivered and he wrapped his great wings around her, shielding her from the light, misty rain and keeping her warm by pressing her to his body.

"He knew no better. He believed me to be cursed, and he was right. But to Morwenna, I was still her older brother, the one who had kissed her scrapes and bruises away. She and her sisters in the Order came to save me. They carried me off and back to their cloister. For years I sat atop the steeple tower, where they protected me by day… and I protected and provided for them at night. As the world progressed, I realized my being there endangered them, so I left."

"Where did you go? What did you do?"

She couldn't help wrapping her arms around his waist and laying her head against his chest, listening to the sound of his heartbeat. There was something so right about being in Holden's arms. There was no place safer, no place she'd rather be. But he was some kind of monster. But could a true monster hold her the way he did, make love to her over and over? And he didn't seem to mind that she had curves, was short, and kept her hair in a spiked pixie cut. Would it be so bad if he really was a gargoyle?

CHAPTER 18

He held her close, trying to memorize this time with her. It didn't matter if she was asking about his past. It didn't matter how kind he was to her or how many orgasms he gave her. What mattered was that he'd lied to her from the beginning. It didn't matter that his feelings for her were the only truth he really believed in. She would never believe she could trust him again, and he didn't blame her. Perhaps he'd left behind the arrogance of his youth, but it seemed instead he'd become a coward. He hadn't been willing to tell her the truth, to let her choose for herself, and risk losing her.

Instead, he had lied to her. He had tried to bind her to him in as many ways as he could and tried to take her choice away. Mazie deserved a better man than that. She might never speak to him beyond tonight, but he would watch over her always. He would ensure that no other evil, no other unclean thing ever touched her again.

They said nothing more. Mazie had stopped shivering, and he folded his wings and tucked them away. He wouldn't force her to look on his misshapen form ever again. She walked to the edge of the roof. He'd known she was afraid of heights. He'd planned to take her to a tall cliff somewhere, or maybe an abandoned castle with a high wall. He'd strip her naked and fuck her to the point where her fear would become adrenaline and her adrenaline turned to lust. He would fuck her so long and so hard that all she would remember was how he'd made her feel, how she'd screamed his name as he pleasured her. It would have worked too, for Mazie's ability to revel in her pleasure was greater than any fear.

He wrapped his arms around her, her back to his front, and stood holding her. The moon was full tonight. Between that and the starry sky, he could almost believe they were far away from the city and far from whoever wanted to hurt her. He would get Rook to pull out of the game. He'd take them both out of the line of fire. He'd give each of them their share of the prize—more if they'd let him.

Holden would never be sure what it was that caught his eye initially, he only knew that as they gazed across the street from the Savoy and away from the Thames, he saw a red beam and a dot appear on Mazie's chest.

"No!" he shouted. He wrapped his arms around her and pulled her underneath him as he dove for cover with her in his arms. A single bullet crashed into his shoulder.

He sucked in air, trying to push down the pain. He didn't care what century it was or what the bullet looked like, the damn things hurt when they entered his body. He rolled with her until they were pressed against a large HVAC unit with his body shielding hers. He realized Mazie wasn't tense, she was alert and aware, but her body was soft and accepted him. She trusted him. Deep down she knew he was her Master and she trusted him to ensure their safety.

The access door opened, and out walked a figure dressed in black, carrying what looked to be a SIG Sauer. He was between them and the only exit off the roof.

"Mazie, they've got us trapped."

"I saw him. We know there's at least two of them, which is more than we knew before. If you think about it, it's been a night of revelations."

They were very much in danger of being killed and she was making jokes?

Holden spoke quietly into her ear. "The only way off this roof is for me to distract the guy with the SIG. I'll draw him away from the door. You get off this roof and get the cops. I'll try to ensure at least this one doesn't get away."

"No can do."

He looked at her, startled by her cavalier attitude and sassy mouth.

"What do you mean 'no can do?'"

"You're either not my Master anymore, in which case you don't get to tell me what to do, or you still are, in which case I'm not going anywhere."

"If I'm still your Master, you will do what I tell you."

"Not necessarily true. I will obey you or face consequences. I'm not leaving you, Holden. Whatever we're going to do, we're going to do it together."

"That staircase is the only way off the roof. We've got to get past that guy."

"That is so not true. You have wings, can't you just fly us away? I'm tempted to say something derogatory about my weight, but I rather imagine I'm already in enough trouble for that teensy weensy outburst downstairs and my unwillingness to let you sacrifice yourself for me."

"Yes, at this point I'd be very careful how you deal with your Master. I see a spanking horse and a stout strap in your future."

"So, we're agreed then that we have a future."

"Keep in mind, I'm immortal, which means you can't even look forward to me dying and being free of me."

"I'm going to hold you to that. Now get us out of here."

Holden grabbed a piece of pipe—he wondered if

management knew how much trash was just lying around up on the rooftop. He tossed the pipe toward one edge of the roof, to direct the attention of the two gunmen in the opposite direction of where he wanted to go. As the one gunman on the roof with them began to run to where the sound of the shot had come, Holden scooped Mazie up in his arms and made a mad dash for the edge of the building, unfurling his wings as he did so.

He leapt over the barrier that ran along the perimeter of the roof that kept things from rolling off and prevented people from falling to their deaths. They started to drop. He knew Mazie had to be terrified, but she never said a word and kept her body lithe and supple. Holden let the wind catch his wings and lift them upward, beating them in a long, strong rhythm and lifting them up into the night sky.

∽

Mazie had been terrified at the idea of Holden leaping off the roof and using his wings to fly them to safety, but then she focused on her breathing to keep her body as relaxed as she could. She wanted to scream when he dove over the side of the building. But the minute they left the roof, it was as if everything fell into place. She trusted Holden. She loved him and whatever this life was going to bring, whatever challenges they faced, they would do so together. And if he ever lied to her again, she was going to rip his balls off. No wait, she liked those things. Okay, she'd gouge his eyes out. No wait, she liked those too. As she mentally listed all his various body parts, she knew the most damage she would ever do to him was perhaps kick him in the shins or stomp on his instep.

She only hoped he could find a way to forgive the hurt she had caused his heart. Granted, finding out your Dom and lover wasn't quite human was a bit to take in, but he would maintain that using foul language and running away from him was not the way to handle it. And he would be right. As soon as she was able, she would show him she was serious.

They soared through back streets and alleys, Holden avoiding the ambient light of the city as well as the bright moonlight. He kept them safe in the dark shadows that he seemed to know so well. Finally, he was able to spiral them down into the close cover of the trees that populated Hyde Park. He found a particularly dense grouping that would be protected from the prying eyes of those who strolled on the beaten footpaths. He landed with a deftness of skill that should have surprised her, but it didn't.

He fished his mobile out of his back pocket. "Phone Holmes. Tell him about the guys on the roof."

She was dialing. "Do you think he knows about you?"

"If he didn't before, he probably does now. That

group is pretty tight knit. I can't see them lying or keeping things from each other."

"Holmes? It's Mazie. Before you go off on me, I'm with Holden."

"Saoirse and Spense said..."

"I don't much care what Saoirse and Spense said. I'm with Holden in Hyde Park. And two guys just tried to shoot us back at the Savoy. One was on the roof of the building across the back of the Savoy. The other had a handgun and was on the roof. Unless he had a key card with the proper access code, once that door closed, he was stuck."

"Okay but tell him I know and we're working on a cover story. The two of you need to stay put and out of sight if you can. Will you do that for me?"

"Yes, I'll tell him."

Mazie ended the call and handed the phone back to him. "What did he say?"

"He said he knows and for us to stay put where we are, if we can. He said they'll get the gunmen and will come up with a cover story. Do you think there's something odd about that group? Holmes seemed very nonplussed by the fact that you're a gargoyle."

"You seem to have gotten over it. I mean to hold you to what you said up on the roof."

"I'm a flexible girl. Besides, you seem willing to forgive me my bad temper… You do forgive me, don't you?"

"I do. I think finding out your Dom once again

wasn't completely honest with you is probably just cause for acting out. I'm not going to lie to you again. Saoirse wants to see if she can't find a way to reverse the curse. I don't know that she can, and I don't know what will happen if she's able to pull it off."

"Well, if we're not sure that you won't die if she does, I vote for remaining a gargoyle. I don't care what you are. I know how you are and who you are to me."

He smiled. "I love you, little one." Holden scanned the sky, and a frown came over his face. "The dawn is approaching."

Mazie could see no trace of morning as she too looked up. "How do you know?"

"After close to seven hundred years, trust me, I know. I want you to call Holmes back. Have him either come for you or send someone he trusts to pick you up. I want you to stay at the Savoy until I come for you tonight. Before you go to bed, I want you to opt the Phantom Guild out of the game."

"Why did you enter? You don't need the money."

"I thought it would be fun to see what the game designers had cooked up. I'll make sure Bishop's family gets his share and pay you and Rook your percentage too."

"Pay Bishop and Rook. I already got what I wanted."

"What's that?" he said, as his lower limbs turned

to stone and the transformation from man to granite gargoyle began to take hold.

She smiled. She wanted the last thing that he saw before he was consumed by the rock to be her smiling face. "You."

CHAPTER 19

*H*olden's mind clicked on, and he knew night was falling. Soon he would be free and could fly to Mazie. He was going to strip them both naked, toss her on the bed, and fall on her like a starving man being offered a buffet. With no preliminaries he would shove up into her and pound on her all night long.

As the last of the granite crumbled and the world came back into focus, he could detect her scent in the air. The smell of her arousal was sweeter than any perfume. He looked down to find Mazie, completely naked, kneeling before him. He glanced up to ensure that she couldn't be seen. He'd chosen a dense clump of trees and foliage. She was on her knees, her hands on her thighs with her palms up. He knew some men got off on long hair falling forward like a veil around their sub's face, but nothing had ever been as exquisite as the sight before him now. She was exposed in a way those other subs never could be. Nothing was hidden from his sight.

He'd seen countless submissives in his time, all waiting for him to take charge and show them what truly great sex was. This was different. This was Mazie and it meant something—not just to him, but also to her. She might be short in stature, but she towered over any who had come before in the way she made him feel. She was soft and curvy with large breasts, a smaller waist that curved outward into full hips he knew he could hang onto when he fucked her as hard as he wanted. She never demurred, never told him to be gentle with her. In fact, she never told him anything except how good he made her feel. And given the number of orgasms she'd had, he knew it wasn't just something she said.

"My beautiful submissive, waiting for my command."

"Yes, Master," she said without lifting her head.

"I don't suppose there's any chance you called Holmes to come get you."

"No, Master, but I did call him to check in and let him know we were safe. They got both guys and he said they're each doing their best to incriminate the other one. Eddy was right, they were running the Baskerville Brigade remotely through zombies."

"Care to tell me why you disobeyed me?"

"Because I wasn't about to leave you here unprotected during the day."

"This is not my normal place of rest, and I was vulnerable. Did you figure out how to get us out of the game?"

"Yes, Sir. I also called Rook and let her know and located Bishop's solicitor."

"You've been busy."

"Yes, Sir."

"I think you're going to have to forfeit your share of the prize."

"I don't mind, Sir. It's an awful lot of money. My little place is fine as long as you'll be in it with me."

"No, I'm afraid it's much too small. I say we start house hunting. Something with a nice large garden where I can rest during the day. We'll host a collaring ceremony at Baker Street, and by this time tomorrow night you'll be wearing my collar and an engagement ring. We can hold the wedding at our home. How does that sound?"

"Wonderful," she said, her eyes glistening with unshed tears. "Where will you be during the day tomorrow?"

"Up in the spirals of Westminster. I've been safe there since the time of Queen Victoria. It will keep me until we can find that house." He held his hand out to her. "Rise, little one."

There was a slight chill to the air and goosebumps were raised all along her flesh. Her nipples were pebbled and hard. She was gorgeous. His hand came up to cup her breast, squeezing and kneading it. He loved the way she moaned and tried to keep still but couldn't quite pull it off. He stood facing her and brought his other hand up to do the same to her other breast. He pinched both of her nipples before giving them a hard tug. They stiffened even more, inviting him to suckle.

When he leaned over, Mazie arched her back, lifting herself so that he could get to her more easily. Her body trembled as he sucked her rhythmically, moving from one nipple to the other and back again. She started to rub her thighs together to give herself some relief and he swatted her backside.

"I told you. I'm in charge of your orgasms. You do not get to play with yourself. It's in the contract."

"I would respectfully remind you, Sir, that I have no contract and no collar and therefore am under no obligation."

He gave her sensitized buds the sharp edge of his teeth and she groaned. "Care to brat off at me some more?"

"No, Sir."

Holden worked his way up her throat, kissing the hollow of her neck, nuzzling her ear, and kissing along her jawline before reaching her mouth. He covered it with his own and thrust his tongue inside. He pulled her close as he bent her backward, forcing her body onto his hard cock as it throbbed between them, and she reached up to grab his shoulders to steady herself.

He slipped his hand between her legs, teasing her clit before moving on to her wet pussy and fingering her, sliding in and out. His fingers came back up to tease her clit, never quite giving her what she needed to come.

"I think this is the way you should greet me each time I awaken. Naked and on your knees before me. Can you do that for me?"

"Yes, Master."

"Good girl. Then put your clothes on and we'll get going."

Her eyes snapped open, "What?"

He chuckled and leaned down to kiss the tip of her nose. "You don't get to disobey me without there being some consequences. Don't look so disappointed. We're going back to the Savoy, order room service, and then I'm going to spend the rest of the night between your legs."

And he did just that, reveling in her embrace and exhausting both of them.

It was two months later, and they'd be meeting 'the gang,' as he liked to call them, for a late supper. Mazie now wore his collar around her neck and his ring around her finger. She had located a beautiful home for them in Belgravia. A late Georgian estate with a small but private garden, where each morning he took up his spot as the curse claimed him. And each night when he awoke, Mazie greeted him as she had that night in Hyde Park—naked and on her knees, ready to service him in whatever way he desired.

She waited for him, only this time she wasn't naked, she wasn't on her knees... and she wasn't alone.

"Problem?" he asked, retracting his wings and slipping on the sweater Mazie handed him. He leaned down and kissed her lightly but thoroughly.

"No. Saoirse thinks she's found it," said Mazie.

Holden's head came up, his eyes searching for and finding the Irish witch, who nodded and smiled.

"The problem is," said Saoirse, "we need to be where the spell was cast. Then we can light the bonfire and I'll reverse the spell. You will become wholly human again, but it might revert you to what would be your natural age."

"Which means I would be dead," he mused.

"No," said Mazie. "We're fine like we are."

"Saoirse, how sure are you it won't kill me?"

"I'd say the odds are probably seventy-five to one in your favor."

"We'll risk it." He raised his hand. "Trust me and trust Saoirse to do this for us."

"We need to do this at the exact opposite time of day from when you were cursed. In other words, if it happened at sunrise, we will do it at sunset."

"It was just after sunset."

"Then we will do it just before sunrise. If we leave now, we can be ready to try it in the morning, and you may never turn to stone again."

Holden nodded. "Can I ask you to bring the roadster? If I'm to lose my wings, I would like to fly with Mazie one last time."

Flying with her in his arms had become a great joy of his. They usually drove out to the countryside and then he would pull her up in his arms and let her experience what it was like to fly without a tin tube surrounding her. He was always grateful for the nights there was extensive cloud cover. He could soar so high above the clouds and not be seen.

Holmes and Rachel drove them out to where they would be unseen. Holden allowed his wings to unfurl for what he hoped was the last time. Sweeping her up in his arms, Holden beat his wings and lifted them into the sky. He climbed higher than normal, as he didn't want to take the chance that they would be seen.

They crossed the English countryside in less than half the time it would have taken to drive it. Holden dipped down along the coastline, allowing her to run her toes along the crashing waves or trail her fingers along the tops of the snowcapped peaks. He loved watching her enjoy what had become mundane to him. Mazie made everything right—bright, shiny, and new.

Holden flew them up along the side of the cliffs

until he landed in what had once been the great bailey of Castle Tremayne.

"This is where you were born," she said, beginning to wander around. "Does it make you sad to see it in this disrepair?"

"A little, although it was never a place of great happiness for me. Mostly I remember all the losses. My mother, who died in childbirth so my father could have a third son. Morwenna kissing me goodbye as she escaped a loveless marriage and my father's evil clutches, the girl falling from the cliff."

Mazie wrapped her arms around him. "It wasn't your fault. She was overwhelmed."

"I should have done something more than reject her and send her away."

"I love you," she said, wrapping her arms around him from the back. "You don't have to do this."

"I do. I have paid my penance long enough. I am a far different man than I was back then, or than I would have been."

They began to gather wood and by the time the others had arrived, the bonfire had been built and all it needed was the strike of a match to set it ablaze.

Saoirse got out of the roadster. She and Spense had driven it down so that Mazie and Holden could have it to drive home. Holden had owned the silver and black 1937 Rolls Royce Phantom III from the first day it was completed.

"I think Holden needs to stand off by himself in

case this thing goes wrong," said Saoirse. Everyone save Mazie moved away from him. "I don't suppose…"

"You would suppose correctly." Mazie turned to Holden. "And don't you start on me."

"Careful little one. We are amongst friends who would not find it untoward of me to spank your pretty backside."

Saoirse lit the bonfire and turned to Holden, raising her arms above her head. She began to intone:

> He who failed her sister sworn
> And caused her family so to mourn
> Has paid his debt and come to the Light
> And will end the curse that plagued his life

Fingers of serpentinite began to come up from the ground below, entwining Holden's feet and then his ankles. Saoirse reversed the counter spell, and the rock began to slow and then stop. As she gave voice to it a third time, the stone began to recede until it had retreated back into the ground completely.

Mazie came to stand in front of him, her back to his front as he wound his arms around her, resting his chin on her head. Surrounded by their friends, they watched as the sun began to rise on a new day and on a new future for them all.

Thank you for reading. **RELEASE is the finale book to the Masters of the Savoy series.**

And if you enjoyed RELEASE, you'll love the Masters of Valor series. The prequel novella, PROPHECY is free.
"Intense, exciting and fast paced." Reviewer

DOWNLOAD PROPHECY FOR FREE

Turn the page for a First Look into **Prophecy**

I have some free bonus content for you! Sign up for my newsletter https://www.subscribepage.com/VIPlist22019. There is a special bonus scene, just for my subscribers. Signing up will also give you access to free books, plus let you hear about sales, exclusive previews and new releases first.

If you enjoyed this book we would love if you left a review, they make a huge difference for indie authors.

As always, my thanks to all of you for reading my books.

Take care of yourselves and each other.

. . .

In case you missed any of the books, here they are:

Masters of the Savoy

Advance

Negotiation

Submission

Contract

Bound

Release

FIRST LOOK

Prologue

Once known as the Knights of the Round Table, fate had forced their hand and they'd watched their chance to be the defenders of the Light slip away. Thirteen original swords had been forged for those who sat at King Arthur's table. Now, only four remain.

Paris, France
Several Months Ago

Gabriel Watson thanked the powers that guided his life for the woman who lay asleep in his arms. He didn't understand how she got here, or how some of his best friends from the Savoy had come into being, but he didn't care. All that mattered was that Anne Hastings, who'd once been known as Anne Boleyn, lay asleep and replete in his arms. A feeling of absolute joy and satisfaction washed over him.

Earlier that day he'd stood at the end of the aisle as the harp had struck the first notes of Mendelssohn's Wedding March and watched the woman he loved with all his heart and soul walk forward and agree to be his wife. It had occurred to him as he took his vows that he'd never planned to marry, much less to an older woman, especially one almost five centuries his senior, but so much of his life seemed to have been ruled by happenstance.

Ten years ago, he'd been pinned down by the enemy with his Marine Raider unit. There were four of them: Tristan Crawford, Bennett Greyson, Ford Montgomery, and himself. They'd pledged their lives and their fortunes to one another as they'd struggled to survive. And they'd held to that vow.

But Gabe was a man caught between three secrets, all of which were about to collide. He'd preached to Anne over and over again about the importance of honesty and transparency in a D/s relationship. But he wasn't walking the walk…

"Gabe, what is it?" she whispered as she lay next to him.

He'd wanted to find the right time, but the text two days ago had changed his need to tell her from the right time to right now. In the archives of texts sent, on the surface this particular text would appear not that momentous, but Gabe knew different.

We've assembled the other swords. Are you with us?

The answer to those two sentences had always been yes, but he'd thought he'd have more time. Time to tell her—to prepare her—that he was about to disrupt their lives completely.

"You need to know that I always meant to tell you, but there wasn't enough time. We swore never to hide things from one another. I need to be honest about something I probably should have explained before we got married…"

"Gabe, whatever it is, it'll be fine. Wait, maybe not. If you're about to tell me that in another life you were Henry VIII, I swear I will cut your balls off, shove them down your throat, and watch you choke on them."

Watson looked down at her incredulously. Even in the dark, he could see her eyes dancing with merriment and her lips curl into the wicked grin he'd come to know so well. Leave it to Anne to make him chuckle when he was feeling as though his back was against the wall. It might well be, but Anne was with him. When he'd faced down two supernatural beings, one of them being the Angel of Death, she'd had to be torn from his side and carried away to safety kicking and screaming.

"If that's the only thing that's going to be an issue for you, we're good."

"It's the sword, isn't it?"

ABOUT THE AUTHOR

Other books by Delta James: <https://www.deltajames.com/>

As a USA Today bestselling romance author, Delta James aims to captivate readers with stories about complex heroines and the dominant alpha males who adore them. For Delta, romance is more than just a love story; it's a journey with challenges and thrills along the way.

After creating a second chapter for herself that was dramatically different than the first, Delta now resides in Virginia where she relaxes on warm summer evenings with her lovable pack of basset hounds as they watch the birds of prey soaring overhead and the fireflies dancing in the fading light. When not crafting fast-paced tales, she enjoys horseback riding, hiking, and white-water rafting.

Her readers mean the world to her, and Delta tries to interact personally to as many messages as she can. If you'd like to chat or discuss books, you can find Delta on Instagram, Facebook, and in her private reader group https://www.facebook.com/groups/348982795738444.

If you're looking for your next bingeable series, you can get a FREE story by joining her newsletter https://www.subscribepage.com/VIPlist22019.

ALSO BY DELTA JAMES

Masters of Valor

Prophecy

Illusion

Deception

Inheritance

Masters of the Savoy

Advance

Negotiation

Submission

Contract

Bound

Release

Fated Legacy

Touch of Fate

Touch of Darkness

Touch of Light

Touch of Fire

Touch of Ice

Touch of Destiny

Syndicate Masters

[The Bargain](#)

[The Pact](#)

[The Agreement](#)

[The Understanding](#)

Masters of the Deep

[Silent Predator](#)

[Fierce Predator](#)

[Savage Predator](#)

[Wicked Predator](#)

Ghost Cat Canyon

[Determined](#)

[Untamed](#)

[Bold](#)

[Fearless](#)

[Strong](#)

[Boxset](#)

Tangled Vines

[Corked](#)

[Uncorked](#)

[Decanted](#)

[Breathe](#)

[Full Bodied](#)

[Late Harvest](#)

Boxset 1

Boxset 2

Mulled Wine

Wild Mustang

Hampton

Mac

Croft

Noah

Thom

Reid

Box Set #1

Box Set #2

Wayward Mates

In Vino Veritas

Brought to Heel

Marked and Mated

Mastering His Mate

Taking His Mate

Claimed and Mated

Claimed and Mastered

Hunted and Claimed

Captured and Claimed

Printed in Great Britain
by Amazon